Exploring Hands-On Science Projects

Experimenting with Sound Science Projects

Robert Gardner

Enslow Publishers, Inc.
40 Industrial Road
Box 398
Berkeley Heights, NJ 07922
USA

http://www.enslow.com

Original edition published as *Science Projects About Sound* in 2000.

Library of Congress Cataloging-in-Publication Data

Gardner, Robert, 1929–
    [Science projects about sound]
    Experimenting with sound science projects / Robert Gardner.
        p. cm.   – (Exploring hands-on science projects)
    Previously published as: Science projects about sound. c2000.
    Summary: "Learn about sound waves, sound and music, the properties of sound and more"–
Provided by publisher.
    Includes bibliographical references and index.
    ISBN 978-0-7660-4148-6
    1. Sound–Experiments–Juvenile literature. I. Title.
QC225.2.G37 2013
534.078–dc23
                                                2012010147

Future editions:
Paperback ISBN: 978-1-4644-0225-8
Single-User PDF ISBN: 978-1-4646-1137-7

EPUB ISBN: 978-1-4645-1137-0
Multi-User PDF ISBN: 978-0-7660-5766-1

Printed in the United States of America

012013 The HF Group, North Manchester, IN

10 9 8 7 6 5 4 3 2 1

To Our Readers: We have done our best to make sure all Internet addresses in this book were active and appropriate when we went to press. However, the author and the publisher have no control over and assume no liability for the material available on those Internet sites or on other Web sites they may link to. Any comments or suggestions can be sent by e-mail to comments@enslow.com or to the address on the back cover.

Photo Credits: Enslow Publishers, Inc., pp. 39, 41, 45, 48, 49, 54, 71, 91, 109, 111; Stephen F. Delisle, pp. 20, 23, 27, 28, 31, 35, 42, 50, 58, 59, 63, 66, 67, 81, 82, 84, 86, 100, 102, 113, 116, 120, 121.

Cover Photo: Shutterstock.com

Contents

CHAPTER 1

MAKING SOUNDS AND NOISES   17

CHAPTER 2

WAVES: A MODEL FOR SOUND   38

CHAPTER 3

MORE ABOUT WAVES   56

CHAPTER 4

PROPERTIES OF SOUND   69

Indicates experiments that offer ideas for science fair projects.

CHAPTER 5

FROM HOSE TELEPHONES TO SOUND EFFECTS

CHAPTER 6

THE SOUNDS OF MUSIC

⊙Indicates experiments that offer ideas for science fair projects.

Introduction

This book is filled with projects and experiments related to sound, from noises that grate the nerves to music that soothes the soul. You will find that you can learn a lot about sound by doing experiments. Most of the materials you will need to carry out your investigations can be found in your home, a hardware store, or a supermarket. For a few experiments, you may want to borrow an item or two from your school's science department. If the school's policy prevents your teachers from letting you take equipment home, you can probably carry out these experiments at school during free time.

For some of the experiments, you will need one or more people to help you. It would be best if you work with friends or adults who enjoy experimenting as much as you do. In that way, you will all enjoy what you are doing. **If any experiment involves the risk of injury, it will be clearly stated in the text. In some cases, to avoid any danger, you will be asked to work with an adult.** Please do so. We do not want you to take any chances that could cause you injury or pain.

Like a good scientist, you will find it useful to record your ideas, notes, data, and anything you can conclude from your experiments in a notebook. By doing so, you can keep track of the information you gather and the conclusions you reach. Record keeping will allow you to refer to experiments you have done that may help you in doing other projects in the future. In some of the experiments, you will have to make some calculations. Therefore, you may find it helpful to have a pocket calculator nearby as you do these experiments and analyze the data you collect.

SCIENCE FAIRS

Some of the projects in this book may be appropriate for a science fair. Those projects are indicated with an asterisk (*). However, judges at such fairs do not reward projects or experiments that are simply copied from a book. For example, plugging numbers into a formula you do not understand will not impress judges. A graph of data collected from experiments you have done that is used to find a relationship between two variables would be more likely to receive serious consideration.

Science fair judges tend to reward creative thought and imagination. It is difficult to be creative or imaginative unless you are really interested in your project. Consequently, you should be sure to choose a subject that appeals to you. And before you jump into a project, consider, too, your own talents and the cost of materials you will need.

If you decide to use a project found in this book for a science fair, you should find ways to modify or extend it. This should not be difficult, because you will probably discover that as you do these projects, new ideas for experiments will come to mind—experiments that could make excellent science fair projects, particularly because the ideas are your own and are interesting to you.

If you decide to enter a science fair and have never done so before, you should read some of the books listed in the Further Reading. These books deal specifically with science fairs and will provide plenty of helpful hints and lots of useful information that will enable you to avoid the pitfalls that sometimes plague first-time entrants. You will learn how to prepare appealing reports that include charts and graphs, how to set up and display your work, how to present your project, and how to relate to judges and visitors.

SAFETY FIRST

Most of the projects included in this book are perfectly safe. However, the following safety rules are well worth reading before you start any project.

1. Do any experiments or projects, whether from this book or of your own design, under the supervision of a science teacher or other knowledgeable adult.
2. Read all instructions carefully before proceeding with a project. If you have questions, check with you supervisor before going any further.
3. Maintain a serious attitude while conducting experiments. Fooling around can be dangerous to you and to others.
4. Wear approved safety goggles when you are working with a flame or doing anything that might cause injury to your eyes.
5. Do not eat or drink while experimenting.
6. Have a first-aid kit nearby while you are experimenting.
7. Do not put your fingers or any object other than properly designed electrical connectors into electrical outlets.
8. Never experiment with household electricity except under the supervision of a knowledgeable adult.
9. Do not touch a lit high-wattage bulb. Lightbulbs produce heat as well as light.
10. Many substances are poisonous. Do not taste them unless instructed to do so.
11. If a thermometer breaks, inform your adult supervisor. Do not touch either the mercury or broken glass with your bare hands.

The Scientific Method

How Scientists Search for Answers

When scientists have a question to answer, they start by researching. They read scientific literature and consult online science databases that are maintained by universities, research centers, or the government. There, they can study abstracts—summaries of reports—by scientists who have conducted experiments or done similar research in the field.

In this way, they find out whether other scientists have examined the same question or have tried to answer it by doing an experiment. Careful research will tell what kind of experiments, if any, have been done to try to answer the question.

Scientists don't want to repeat experiments that have known and accepted outcomes. Also, they want to avoid repeating any mistakes others may have made while doing similar experiments. If no one else has done scientific work that answers the question, scientists then do further research on how best to do the experiment.

While researching for the experiment, the scientist tries to guess—or predict—the possible results. This prediction is called a hypothesis.

The scientist hopes that a well-researched and carefully planned experiment will prove the hypothesis to be true. At times, however, the results of even the best-planned experiment can be far different from what the scientist expected. Yet even if the results indicate the hypothesis was not true, this does not mean the experiment was a failure. In fact, unexpected results can provide valuable information that leads to a different answer or to another, even better, experiment.

Using the Scientific Method in Experiments and Projects

The Scientific Method

A scientific experiment starts when someone wonders what would happen if certain conditions were set up and tested by following a specific process. For example, in an experiment testing the ability of table salt (sodium chloride) to conduct electricity, you can ask the question: "Is table salt more conductive when it is dissolved in water to make a saltwater solution?"

To find the answer, some possible guesses, hypotheses, would be:

- Solid table salt conducts electricity better than saltwater.

- Saltwater conducts electricity better than solid table salt.

- Neither form of table salt will conduct electricity.

Let's say your hypothesis is that salt water will conduct electricity better than the solid table salt. For a start, we have to know that a scientific experiment can have only two variables—that is, only two things that can change. For this experiment, one variable is whether the salt is dissolved in water or whether it is solid. The other variable will be the electrical conductivity of each form of salt.

The form of salt is allowed to change (either a solid or in solution) but not the equipment producing the electrical charge, and not the amount or strength of the charge the equipment produces. If the electrical charge differed when the solid salt and the salt solution were tested, then we couldn't tell how the conductivity of one form compared to the other.

Now, if the experiment is carried out and the results show there is no difference in the conductivity of solid salt and dissolved salt, this would not mean your experiment is a failure. Even if your hypothesis—dissolved salt conducts electricity better—turns out to be false, the results of your experiment still can provide important information. And these results may lead to further ideas that can be explored.

Scientists may develop logical explanations for the results of their experiments. These explanations, or theories, then must be tested by more experiments. If the resulting data from more experiments provide compelling support for a theory, then that theory could be accepted by the world of science. But scientists are careful about accepting new theories. If the resulting data contradict a theory, then the theory must be discarded, altered, or retested. That is the scientific method.

Basic Steps in the Scientific Method

The best experiments and science projects usually follow the scientific method's basic steps:

- Ask questions about what would happen if certain conditions or events were set up and tested in an experiment.

- Do background research to investigate the subject of your questions until you have a main question.

- Construct a hypothesis—an answer to your question—that you can then test and investigate with an experiment.

- Design and conduct an experiment to test your hypothesis.

- Keep records, collecting data, and then analyze what you've recorded.

- Draw a conclusion based on the experiment and the data you've recorded.

- Write a report about your results.

Your Hypothesis

Many experiments and science projects begin by asking whether something can be done or how it can be done. How do you search for an answer? Form your hypothesis? First, read about your topic. After your research, you might make an educated guess in answer to the question; this is your hypothesis. You'll also find out what methods, materials, and equipment are needed to design an experiment that tests your hypothesis.

Remember: To give your experiment or project every chance of success, prepare a hypothesis that is clear and brief. The simpler the better.

Designing the Experiment

Your experiment will be structured to investigate whether the hypothesis is true or false. The experiment is intended to test the hypothesis, not necessarily to prove that the hypothesis is right.

The results of a well-designed experiment are more valuable than the results of an experiment that is intentionally designed to give the answer you want. The conditions you set up in your experiment must be a fair test of your hypothesis.

By carefully carrying out your experiment you'll discover useful information that can be recorded as data (observations). It's most important that the experiment's procedures and results are as accurate as possible. Design the experiment for observable, measurable results. And keep it simple, because the more complicated your experiment is, the more chance you have for error.

Also, if you have friends helping you with an experiment or project, make sure from the start that they'll take their tasks seriously.

Remember: Scientists around the world always use metric measurements in their experiments and projects, and so should you. Use metric liquid and dry measures and a Celsius thermometer.

Recording Data

Your hypothesis, procedure, data, and conclusions should be recorded immediately as you experiment, but don't keep it on loose scraps of paper. Record your data in a notebook or logbook—one you use just for experiments. Your notebook should be bound so that you have a permanent record. The laboratory notebook is an essential part of all academic and scientific research.

Make sure to include the date, experiment number, and a brief description of how you collected the data. Write clearly. If you have to cross something out, do it with just a single line, then rewrite the correct information.

Repeat your experiment several times to be sure your results are consistent and your data are trustworthy. Don't try to interpret data as you go along. It's better first to record results accurately, then study them later.

You might even find that you want to replace your experiment's original question with a new one. For example, by answering the question, "What is the chemical process behind yeast as a leavening agent?" you learn that yeast consumes sugar (glucose).This brings up other questions: "Is there a limit to how much sugar yeast can digest? Can too much sugar inhibit the leavening process?"

Writing the Science Fair Report

Communicate the results of your experiment by writing a clear report. Even the most successful experiment loses its value if the scientist cannot clearly tell what happened. Your report should describe how the experiment was designed and conducted and should state its precise results.

Following are the parts of a science fair report, in the order they should appear:

• The Title Page

The title of your experiment should be centered and near the top of the page. Your teacher will tell you what other information is needed, such as your name, grade, and the name of your science teacher.

• Table of Contents
On the report's second page, list the remaining parts of the report and their page numbers.

• Abstract
Give a brief overview of your experiment. In just a few sentences, tell the purpose of the experiment, what you did, and what you found out. Always write in plain, clear language.

• Introduction
State your hypothesis and explain how you came up with it. Discuss your experiment's main question and how your research led to the hypothesis. Tell what you hoped to achieve when you started the experiment.

• Experiment and Data
This is a detailed step-by-step explanation of how you organized and carried out the experiment. Explain what methods you followed and what materials and equipment you used.

State when the experiment was done (the date and perhaps the time of day) and under what conditions (in a laboratory, outside on a windy day, in cold or warm weather, etc.) Tell who was involved and what part they played in the experiment.

Include clearly labeled graphs and tables of data from the experiment as well as any photographs or drawings that help illustrate your work. Anyone who reads your report should be able to repeat the experiment just the way you did it. (Repeating an experiment is a good way to test whether the original results were obtained correctly.)

• Discussion
Explain your results and conclusions, perhaps comparing them with published scientific data you first read about in

your research. Consider how the experiment's results relate to your hypothesis. Ask yourself: Do my results support or contradict my hypothesis? Then analyze the answer.

Would you do anything differently if you did this experiment again? State what you've learned as a result of the experiment.

Analyze how your tools and equipment did their tasks, and how well you and others used those tools. If you think the experiment could be done better if designed another way or if you've another hypothesis that might be tested, then include this in your discussion.

- **Conclusion**

Make a brief summary of your experiment's results. Include only information and data already stated in the report, and be sure not to bring in any new information.

- **Acknowledgments**

Give credit to everyone who helped you with the experiment. State the names of these individuals and briefly explain who they are and how they assisted you.

- **References / Bibliography**

List any books, magazines, journals, articles, Web sites, scientific databases, and interviews that were important to your research for the experiment.

Science Fairs

Science fair judges tend to reward creative thought and imagination. It's difficult to be creative or imaginative unless you're really interested in your project. So, be sure to choose a subject that appeals to you. And before you jump into a project, consider your own talents and the cost of materials you'll need.

Remember, judges at science fairs don't reward projects or experiments that are simply copied from a book. If you decide to use a project from this book for a science fair, you should find ways to modify or extend it. This

shouldn't be difficult because you'll probably discover that, as you do these projects, new ideas for experiments will come to mind. These experiments could make excellent science fair projects, particularly because the ideas are your own and are interesting to you.

If you decide to enter a science fair and have never done so before, you should read some of the books listed in the Further Reading section and visit the Internet sites. The books and sites with titles that refer to science fairs will provide plenty of helpful hints and information that will help you avoid the pitfalls that sometimes plague first-time entrants. You'll learn how to prepare appealing reports that include charts and graphs, how to set up and display your work, how to present your project, and how to relate to judges and visitors. Following are some suggestions to consider.

Some Tips for Success at a Science Fair

Science teachers and science fair judges have many different opinions on what makes a good science fair project or experiment.

Here are the most important elements:

Originality of Concept is one of the most important things judges consider. Some judges believe that the best science fair projects answer a question that is not found in a science textbook.

Scientific Content is another main area of evaluation. How was science applied in the procedure? Are there sufficient data? Did you stick to your intended procedure and keep good records?

Thoroughness is next in importance. Was the experiment repeated as often as needed to test your hypothesis? Is your notebook complete, and are the data accurate? Does your research bibliography show you did enough library work?

Clarity in how you present your exhibit shows you had a good understanding of the subject you worked on. It's important that your exhibit clearly presents the results of your work.

Effective Process: Judges recognize that how skillfully you carry out a science fair project is usually more important than its results. A well-done project gives students the best understanding of what scientists actually do day-to-day.

Other points to consider when preparing for your science fair:

The Abstract: Write up a brief explanation of your project and make copies for visitors or judges who want to read it.

Knowledge: Be ready to answer questions from visitors and judges confidently. Know what is in your notebook and make some notes on index cards to remind you of important points.

Practice: Before the science fair begins, prepare a list of several questions you think you might be asked. Think about the answers and about how your display can help to support them. Have a friend or parent ask you questions and answer them out loud. Knowing your work thoroughly helps you feel more confident when you're asked about it.

Appearance: Dress and act in a way that shows you take your project seriously. Visitors and judges should get the impression that you're interested in the project and take pride in answering their questions about it.

Remember: Don't block your exhibit. Stand to the side when someone is looking at it.

Some projects have special needs with respect to displays. If you cannot show the experiment or results, photograph or draw them. Show the materials used at the start of the experiment and those produced at the end, if possible, and mount them on a display. Photograph or draw any special tools or setups. Be inventive about different ways of showing what took place.

Chapter 1

Making Sounds and Noises

If you can hear, you know what sound is. You hear sounds all day long, from the time you are awakened by your alarm clock in the morning until silence and fatigue bring a restful night of sleep. You may be surprised to learn that even people who cannot hear sound can feel it. After completing the experiments in this chapter, you will understand how it is possible to feel sound as well as hear it. You will learn, too, how sound is related to vibration (the up and down or back and forth movement of an object), how sound behaves differently in air and in a vacuum (a space that contains nothing, not even air), how sound changes with distance, what is needed to make sound resonate (intensify), and how the sounds emitted by a string are related to the string's length and tension.

To understand sound you need to know what pitch means. High-pitched sounds are the kind made by a soprano (high notes) or the keys on the right side of a piano. Low-pitched sounds are the kind made by a bass singer (low notes), a bass fiddle, or the keys on the left side of a piano.

You also need to know that the air through which sounds travel is made up of tiny particles called molecules. About 78 percent of those particles are nitrogen molecules and 21 percent are oxygen molecules. The rest of the air consists of molecules of several different elements and compounds. All of these molecules are in rapid motion, colliding with one another, with objects in the air, with you, and with your ears. It is the molecules that strike your eardrum that enable you to hear sounds.

Materials:

-long, thin stick, such as a wooden, metal, or plastic ruler or yardstick

-wooden block

-table or bench

-metal strip, such as a hacksaw blade

-plastic, wooden, and metal rulers or plastic, wooden, and metal strips

-a friend

What causes sound? To find out, you might begin by trying to make as many different sounds as possible. What is the common factor in making all these sounds?

Focus your attention on a single noisemaker. You will need a long, thin stick, such as a wooden or plastic ruler or yardstick. Use a wooden block to hold one end of the stick on the edge of a table or bench, as shown in Figure 1. Pluck the end of the stick that projects beyond the table with your free hand. You will see the stick vibrate up and down. Can you hear anything? (Do not mistake the short-lasting sound your finger makes when you pluck the stick from any longer-lasting sounds that the stick may make.)

Make the vibrating part of the stick shorter by moving more of the stick onto the table. Then pluck it again. Can you hear anything now? What happens to the pitch as you continue to make the vibrating stick shorter by small amounts? What happens when you lengthen the stick?

Repeat the experiment with a metal strip, such as a metal ruler. Are the results similar? Are there any differences?

Gather some lengths of different materials: strips of plastic, wood, and metal. At this point you will probably need a friend to help you with an experiment. Your friend can work with one kind of strip while you work with another of the same length. Then you can both produce sounds, one

shortly after the other, and compare what you hear.
If the different strips are the same length, are the
sounds they make the same?

From what you have found in this experiment, what
is at least one way of making sounds? How can the pitch
of a sound be changed? How is the frequency (number of
vibrations per second) at which a stick vibrates related
to the pitch of the sound it produces?

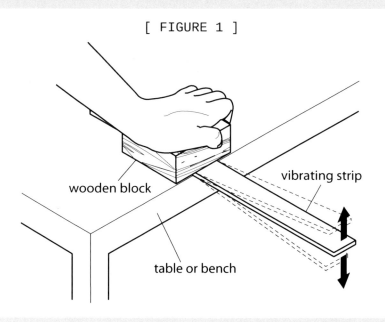

[FIGURE 1]

vibrating strip

wooden block

table or bench

**Does a vibrating stick or rod make a sound? If it does,
is the pitch of the sound related to the frequency of
vibration? Is the frequency of vibration related to the
stick's length?**

EXPLORING ON YOUR OWN

In this experiment, you used a strip held horizontally.
Will the results be different if the strip is held in a
vertical position?

1.2 Other Sources of Vibrations and Sound

Materials:

- -C-clamp
- -length of heavy string
- -old table or bench
- -rubber bands, thick and thin
- -tuning fork
- -balloon
- -scissors
- -2 plastic soda straws
- -paper cup filled with water
- -thread
- -tape
- -Ping-Pong ball

If vibrating sticks make sounds, perhaps other vibrating objects will do so as well. To see if this is so, use a C-clamp to fasten one end of a length of string to the edge of an old table or bench. Pull on the other end of the string to make it tight. Then pluck the string. Can you see the center of the string become blurry as it vibrates? Does it make a sound? What happens if you decrease the tension on the string by loosening it slightly? What happens if you increase the tension on the string by tightening it?

Predict what will happen if you pluck the string and then suddenly tighten the string to increase the tension. Try it! Were you right?

Keeping the tension as constant as possible, predict what effect a shorter length of the same string will have on the pitch of the sound. Try it! Were you right?

Repeat this experiment, using a length of a thick rubber band in place of the string. Does the vibrating rubber band produce a sound? If it does, can you predict what will happen to the pitch as you increase the tension in the rubber band? As you decrease the tension? Can you predict what will happen to the pitch if, without changing the tension, you shorten the band by moving your hand along the band until it is closer to the clamp? Were you right? Try using a thinner rubber band. How is the sound affected by the thickness of the rubber band?

Blow up a balloon. Hold the neck of the balloon in your fingers. Stretch the neck of the balloon by pulling opposite sides outward with your fingers as you release the air. Watch the mouth of the balloon. What do you hear? Are the sounds you hear related to any vibrations you can see?

Use scissors to make narrow triangular cuts in one end of a soda straw, as shown in Figure 2. Chew the flaps that you have formed at the end of the straw until they become flat and flexible. You have made a reed.

Now place your lips just beyond the flaps in the reed so that the flaps are inside your mouth. Blow through the straw gently. Gradually increase the force with which you blow until your hear a sound. What do you think is vibrating to produce the sound?

Place a straw that has *not* been cut into your mouth. Try blowing through this straw in the same way. Do you hear a similar sound? Why not?

Repeat the experiment with the reed, but cut the reed in half. Blow into this shorter reed. What do you notice about the sound you hear? Has the pitch increased or decreased? What does this tell you about the frequency of the vibrations?

Borrow a tuning fork from your school. Hold the base of the tuning fork and hit the tines with a rubber mallet or strike it against the heel of your shoe. Can you hear a sound? Is anything vibrating?

[FIGURE 2]

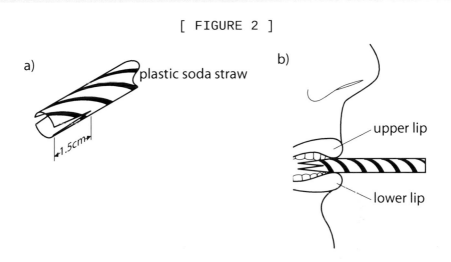

a) You can make a simple reed from a plastic soda straw. Cut triangular pieces from both sides at one end of the straw. Chew the flaps you have made until they are flat and flexible. b) Put your lips beyond the flaps and blow.

Strike the tines of the tuning fork again. Then dip the tines into a paper cup filled with water. What happens? What does this tell you about the tines? What is producing the sound you hear?

Suspend a Ping-Pong ball from a thread with tape and hold it next to one tine of the fork while it is producing a sound. What happens to the ball? What does this tell you about the source of the sound?

1.3 Vibrations, Sound, and Air

Materials:

- steel can, such as a soup can
- can opener
- large balloon
- scissors
- crystals of salt or sugar
- a friend
- towel or cloth
- small table radio

Carefully use a can opener to cut off both the top and bottom of a steel can. Remember that the edges are sharp. **Handle the can so as not to cut yourself.** Blow up and deflate a balloon so that it loses some of its elastic strength. Use scissors to cut off the neck and the third of the balloon closest to the neck. Stretch the remaining two thirds of the balloon over one end of the open steel can. The balloon should be stretched tightly over the can.

Hold the can with the balloon-covered end uppermost while you sprinkle a few crystals of salt or sugar onto the balloon. Ask a friend to lie on the floor. Place a towel or cloth over your friend's eyes to protect them from any crystals that might fall from the balloon. Then hold the open end of the can slightly above your friend's mouth and ask him or her to speak or sing into the can. What happens to the crystals on the balloon? If you do not observe any change, ask your friend to speak louder.

Repeat the experiment with a radio. Place the radio so that its speaker is turned upward. Hold the open mouth of the can near, but not on, the speaker. What happens to the crystals on the balloon when sound enters the can? If nothing happens to the crystals on the surface of the rubber, turn up the radio's volume. How can you explain what is happening to the crystals? How can the vibrations from a person's voice or a radio reach the rubber balloon covering the top of the can?

1.4 Feeling Sound

Materials:
- large balloon
- radio or TV

In Experiment 1.3 you saw how sound can exert a force on crystals some distance from the source of the sound. In this experiment you will find that you can feel the effects of sound with your fingers.

Stretch a large balloon with your hands. Stretching the rubber will make it easier to blow up. Now blow up the balloon so it is at least 20 cm (8 in) in diameter and tie the end. Hold the balloon gently with your fingertips and move it close to your mouth. As you speak or sing, direct your voice toward the balloon. What do you feel in your fingertips? What happens to that feeling when you stop speaking or singing? How can you explain what you felt?

Holding the balloon in the same way, bring it close to the speaker of a radio or TV. What do you feel in your fingertips when sound is coming from the speaker?

Hold your fingertips lightly against your windpipe as you sing a loud note or speak loudly. What do you feel? How can you explain what you feel?

EXPLORING ON YOUR OWN

Carry out an investigation to determine how the speaker in a radio or television set works.

What are woofers and tweeters? How do they differ? How are they the same?

Where are your vocal cords? How do your vocal cords (or folds) allow you to make sounds?

How can sounds be changed to the electrical impulses that make a telephone work?

Materials:

- construction paper
- scissors or shears
- ruler
- transparent plastic tape
- cardboard
- two 2-liter soda bottles
- two 1-liter soda bottles
- piano
- musical instrument other than a piano (optional)
- movie of the Tacoma Narrows Bridge collapse (optional)

Every object that vibrates has a natural rate (frequency) of vibration; that is, it will always vibrate a certain number of times per minute. That natural rate is determined by the object's mass, stiffness, and size. Watch a young child on a swing. The swing moves back and forth with a natural (automatic) frequency that depends on the swing's length. The frequency (number of swings per time) is independent of the amplitude of the swing (the distance it moves) or the weight of the child. If you push the swing each time the child completes one oscillation (vibration) and begins the next, you will increase the amplitude of the swing.

If forces are applied to a vibrating object at times that match its natural frequency, the amplitude of the vibration will increase. When this happens, it is called resonance. The frequency of the applied force need not be identical to the natural frequency of the resonating object. For example, you could push the child on every other oscillation; that is, with a frequency half as great as the natural frequency of the swing. Or you could push on every third or fourth swing, or every half swing if you have a partner who pushes on the other side of the swing.

To see examples of resonance at different frequencies, you can make a series of paper rings. From construction paper, use scissors or shears to cut strips one inch wide. Make the longest one about 50 cm (20 in) long. (If you do not have large sheets of construction paper, you can cut strips from 8 $^1/_2$ × 11-in paper. Then use short, narrow lengths of transparent plastic tape to join shorter strips to make long ones.) The other strips could be about 40 cm, 30 cm, and 15 cm (16 in, 12 in, and 6 in) long. Tape the ends of each strip together to make rings. Then tape the rings to a sheet of cardboard, as shown in Figure 3.

Start at very low frequencies—that is, shake the cardboard slowly back and forth from side to side. You

[FIGURE 3]

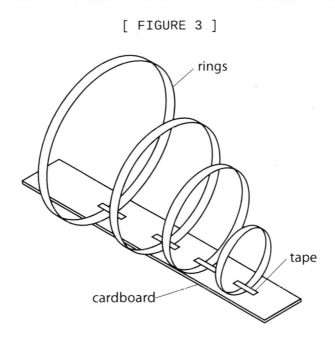

Resonating rings can be made from strips of construction paper that you tape to a sheet of cardboard.

will find that the biggest ring will be the first to begin to resonate. Continue increasing the rate at which you move the cardboard until the smallest ring resonates. Can you make the rings resonate by moving the cardboard up and down?

Resonance with sound is very common. If you blow gently across the mouth of an empty 2-liter soda bottle, you will hear the air inside vibrate at its natural frequency. Now, blow gently across the mouth of the bottle again while holding the open mouth of a second identical bottle near one ear, as shown in Figure 4. Can you hear the sound produced by resonance coming from the bottle next to your ear? We say the air in the second bottle vibrates in sympathy with the air in the first bottle. How does the sound produced in the second bottle compare with the sound you generated in the first bottle?

[FIGURE 4]

Is there evidence of resonance in the bottle near your ear when you blow gently into an identical bottle?

Repeat the experiment, but this time hold the mouth of a 1-liter bottle next to your ear. What do you hear? How can you explain the result?

Predict what you will hear if you repeat this experiment but blow across the mouth of a 1-liter bottle with the mouth of an identical 1-liter bottle next to your ear. Were you right?

Have a friend push his or her foot down on the right-hand pedal of a piano. If possible, look inside the piano when this is done. You will see that the dampers on all the strings are lifted when that pedal is down. All the strings are now free to vibrate. Sing a note into the piano or play a note on another instrument near the piano. Then listen to the piano. Can you hear a string that has been set into sympathetic vibration? What note is produced by the piano string? Do any other strings vibrate? If they do, can you explain why?

When large bridges are built, the architects must be careful not to design a structure that will resonate with the forces exerted by certain wind velocities. In 1940, the Tacoma Narrows Bridge, resonating in response to the wind, vibrated with such large amplitudes that it collapsed and fell into the water below. Your teacher or librarian may know where you can find the short movie that shows the Tacoma Narrows Bridge vibrating and finally collapsing (or search on the Internet).

EXPLORING ON YOUR OWN

Design and carry out a number of experiments to show resonance with sounds.

Where else, besides with sound, can you find examples of resonance? What role does resonance play in tuning a radio?

1.6 Sound, Air, and a Vacuum

Materials:
- electronic buzzer and battery (purchase from an electronics or radio store)
- bell jar
- insulated wires
- switch
- vacuum pump
- a science teacher

Sound seems to be produced by vibrating objects, and since sounds can reach our ears from a distance, sometimes over very large distances, sound must somehow travel through space to reach our ears. Although we are bathed in light from the sun, we do not hear any of the sounds that must be generated on the sun. After all, huge reactions are taking place there, reactions more powerful than the hydrogen bombs developed on earth. Can it be that sound cannot travel through the vacuum of empty space that separates the earth from the sun? Astronauts who have walked in the space outside their spacecraft know they have to communicate with one another by radio. They cannot hear one another even if separated only by short distances. Sound, unlike light, apparently cannot travel through a vacuum.

You can carry out an experiment to see if sound generated in a vacuum can be heard. You will probably need equipment from your school and help from a science teacher to do this. An electronic buzzer and the battery to drive it can be suspended in a bell jar with wires leading to a switch outside the jar. The bell jar can be connected to a vacuum pump, which can pump nearly all the air out of the jar.

[FIGURE 5]

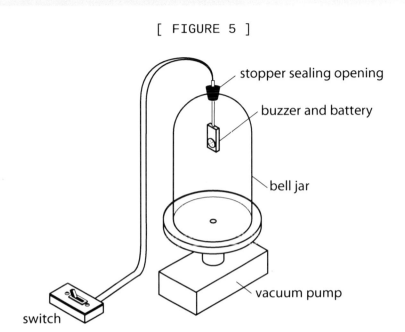

stopper sealing opening

buzzer and battery

bell jar

vacuum pump

switch

What happens to the sound from a buzzer when the air is removed from the space around it?

Under the guidance of your science teacher, set up the apparatus as shown in Figure 5. Turn on the switch so that you hear the buzzer. Then start the pump to remove most of the air from the bell jar. What happens to the sound from the buzzer as air is removed from the space around it?

You know that you can sometimes see people talking even though you cannot hear them. Every football huddle is based on the assumption that the opposing team cannot hear what is being said. You may have noticed professional baseball pitchers covering their mouths when they talk to their catchers. This is not to prevent an opponent from hearing them but from reading their lips.

Materials:
- a friend
- large room with windows
- meterstick, yardstick, or measuring tape
- radio
- clicker
- wind

In your home or school, ask someone to sit in the center of a large room and whisper the same word at the same intensity over and over while you move farther and farther away. How far must you move from the source of the sound before you are unable to hear the word?

Does it matter in what direction you move? For example, can you move farther away and still hear if you stay in front of the person rather than behind him or her? Does it matter whether you move to the left or to the right of the person?

Suppose the person tries to direct the sound by cupping his hand beside his mouth, as those who whisper often do. Can you hear the word from farther away in the direction the person is trying to direct the sound? Is the sound successfully shielded from the opposite direction?

Move to the point where you are first unable to hear the whispered word. Cup your hand next to your ear. In effect, you are increasing the area and depth of your outer ear. Can you hear the whispered word now? If you can, try to explain why you can.

Is your hearing distance affected by open windows? If it is, how is it affected?

Suppose other sounds are present, such as a radio that is playing music. Does the other sound affect the distance that you can hear the whispered word? If so, how does it affect it?

Repeat the experiment outside. Can you hear farther from the source outside than inside? Why, or why not?

Ask a friend to join you in using a clicker outside on a windy day. Does wind affect the distance from which you can hear the clicker? If it does, how does it affect it? Does temperature affect the distance from which you can hear the clicker?

EXPLORING ON YOUR OWN

Design and carry out an experiment to find out how the intensity (loudness) of sound is affected by distance. Does doubling the distance halve the sound's intensity?

Increasing the distance from a point source of light from d to $2d$ reduces the intensity of the light at $2d$ to one fourth its intensity at d. Explain why this is true. Is the same true for sound?

If you live in a climate where it snows in the winter, find out if snow-covered ground affects the distance from which you can hear the clicker. If it does, does it increase or decrease your hearing distance? Can you explain why? Design and carry out an experiment to determine whether it is the snow or the cold temperature that affects the distance from which you can hear the clicker.

Investigate how deaf people communicate by "reading lips." How do they communicate by sign language?

Materials:

- two 1.0-m (3-ft) lengths of 50-pound-test monofilament fishing line
- 2 screw eyes
- 60 cm x 30 cm (2 ft x 1 ft) board
- plastic pails to hold water
- C-clamp
- table
- short length of 3/4-inch, triangular-shaped or quarter-round board (buy at a lumber yard)
- water
- one 1.0-m (3-ft) length of 20-pound-test monofilament fishing line
- measuring cup
- clay

If you have ever seen a symphony orchestra, you must have noticed the great number of stringed instruments near the front of the stage—violins, violas, and cellos. All these stringed instruments and others, such as the guitar, harp, banjo, and mandolin, generate sounds by having their stretched strings plucked or bowed. (A bow is a wooden stick holding a strong, stretched cord that is rubbed across the strings.) The sounds the strings produce are amplified by the sounding boards beneath the strings (see Experiment 4.4).

To find out how the frequency at which a string vibrates is related to its length, tension, and thickness, you can build the device shown in Figure 6. One end of each of two 1.0-m (3-ft) lengths of 50-pound-test monofilament fishing line are tied to the two screw eyes at one end of the 60 cm × 30 cm (2 ft × 1 ft) board. The other ends are tied to small plastic pails that will hold water. Use a C-clamp to fasten the board to a table. Insert a short length of a triangular-shaped piece of wood under each string as shown. If you cannot find a triangular-shaped piece, use

[FIGURE 6]

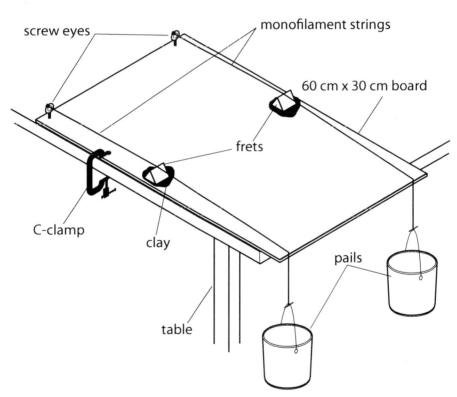

screw eyes

monofilament strings

60 cm x 30 cm board

frets

C-clamp

clay

pails

table

The apparatus shown in the drawing can be used to find out how tension, length, and thickness (string density) affect the pitch (frequency of vibration) of a string.

a short length of $^3/_4$-inch quarter-round (see Figure 6). These short lengths of board that lift the string and serve as end points for the string are called frets. If you use quarter-round board, put pieces of clay on each side of the frets to keep them from wobbling. The string is now free to vibrate between the screw eye and the fret and between the fret and the end of the board.

Fill one pail halfway with water. This will put tension on the string. Now move the fret so that the length of this string between the screw eye and the fret is about half as long as the length of string between the fret and the end of the board. Pluck the short length of string and then pluck the longer length. How do the sounds compare? Which string has the higher pitch? Which string vibrates with the higher frequency? As you can see, the greater the frequency of vibration, the higher the pitch of the note produced by the string.

What do you think you should do to make the two parts of the string vibrate with the same frequency? Do it. Do they now have the same pitch—that is, do they produce the same musical note when you pluck them?

What happens to the pitch of one section of the string when you make it shorter by pressing it against the board with your finger? What happens to the pitch as you make the string longer?

Now, fill the second pail with water. This will put the second string under about twice as much tension as the first string (the one with which you have been working). Remove the frets so that the full lengths of the two strings, both as long as the distance from the screw eyes to the end of the board, are free to vibrate. Pluck first one string and then the other. Watch the two strings carefully as they vibrate. How do their frequencies of vibration compare? Which string has the higher pitch? What effect, if any, does tension have on the frequency at which a string vibrates?

Next, replace one of the strings with a thinner 20-pound-test line. Attach both lines to identical plastic pails. Carefully add equal amounts of water to both pails so that both strings are under the same tension. Pluck both strings. How does the thickness or density (mass per length) of a string affect its frequency of vibration or pitch? What can you do to make both strings produce the same sound when plucked?

EXPLORING ON YOUR OWN

Design and carry out an experiment to determine how a string's frequency of vibration is related to its tension, length, and density (weight per unit length). When you finish experimenting, you should be able to write an equation summarizing the relationship.

Look inside a piano. Notice the differences in the thickness and length of the various strings. Explain how those differences affect the note you hear when you strike different keys with your fingers.

WAVES: A MODEL FOR SOUND

In Chapter 1 you found that sound is produced by vibrating objects. The greater the frequency of the vibrations, the higher the pitch of the sound. You also found that sound can travel through air and exert forces on small particles, such as salt or sugar crystals. By directing sound at a balloon you held with your fingertips, you discovered that you could feel the vibrating air caused by sound. Your fingers tingled when sounds from your vocal cords or a radio or television speaker were directed at the balloon. You could feel similar vibrations when you placed your fingers on your windpipe as you sang or talked. You found, however, as have astronauts, that sound, unlike light and radio signals, cannot travel through a vacuum. For sound to move from its source to your ear, it needs air to carry it. It may be that other media can carry sound as well, but for now we will consider only air as a medium through which sound can travel.

To begin to figure out how sound moves, find out if a large single vibration can be carried by air.

Materials:
- empty one-gallon plastic milk container
- candle
- candleholder
- an adult
- matches

Find an empty one-gallon plastic milk container. Turn the mouth of the container toward your face and hit the center of the bottom of the container with your fist. What did you feel on your face? Can you explain why you felt it?

Next, put a candle in a candleholder and place it on a table. **Under adult supervision**, light the candle. Hold the empty milk container about three feet from the candle, as shown in Figure 7. Aim the mouth of the container at the candle flame. Use your fist to apply a sharp blow to the bottom of the container. If you have aimed the container correctly, the flame will go out. Can you explain why?

With practice, you will find that you can use the milk container to blow out a candle flame from distances of five or six feet.

[FIGURE 7]

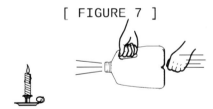

A sharp blow to the bottom of a large empty milk container can put out a candle.

EXPLORING ON YOUR OWN

Stand a soda bottle close to the candle to serve as a shield between the candle and the milk container. When you hit the milk container, you will still be able to extinguish the flame. Can you explain why?

2.2 Multiple Air Pulses and a Molecular Model

Materials:

- 6 or more identical marbles
- grooved ruler
- one-gallon milk container
- masking tape
- pen

As you have seen, a vibration, such as the one you made when you slammed your fist into the milk container, can produce a pulse (a brief disturbance of the level) of air pressure. In Experiment 2.1 you found that such a pulse can be carried through the air from one place to another. If one pulse can be transported by air, there is no reason why many pulses cannot be sent along the same medium.

You can see for yourself that this is true. Take an empty one-gallon milk container and hold its mouth near your face. Then strike the base of the container repeatedly with your free hand. Can you feel repeated pulses of air striking your face?

A Model for the Movement of Sound

Vibrations can produce sound. Vibrations can also produce pulses of air pressure that can travel through the air. It is reasonable to think that the vibrations that produce sound can create multiple pulses of air that can be carried in rapid succession from their source to your ear. But how does the pulse travel through air?

As explained in Chapter 1, air, like all gases, is made up of tiny particles called molecules. Most of the air (78 percent) consists of nitrogen molecules; there are also oxygen molecules (21 percent), and small amounts of other gases such as argon and carbon dioxide.

To show how pulses travel through air, you can use marbles to represent air molecules. Mark about six identical marbles with a letter to identify them. You can write the letters on a small piece of masking tape. Place the marbles a short distance apart on a flat grooved ruler, as shown in Figure 8. The marbles represent undisturbed air molecules. Of course, air molecules are never at rest, but, on the average, they would be moving more slowly than molecules that were hit by a vibrating object. Roll another identical marble that represents an air molecule that has been hit by a vibrating object into the marbles lined up on the ruler. The other marbles represent air molecules that have not been struck by anything. Watch what happens when the moving marble strikes the marble nearest to it. As you can see, the marbles bump into one another in turn. The farthest marble moves with approximately the same speed as the one that you rolled into the others.

[FIGURE 8]

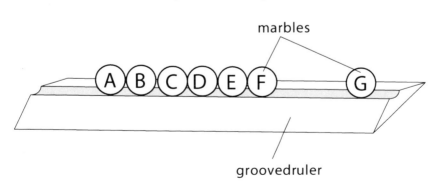

marbles

groovedruler

A pulse of sound can be illustrated by an analogy in which marbles represent air molecules.

The successive bumping of one marble into another is a model for a series of molecular collisions that transmit a pulse of pressure through the air. This demonstration shows how sound reaches your ear. The pressure changes needed to move your eardrum are very small. The human ear is incredibly sensitive. It can detect intensities as small as a trillionth of a watt per square meter. (That is less than the energy involved in a rustling leaf.) Some of those pressure pulses may reach your ear (Figure 9).

The human ear is made up of the outer, middle, and inner ear. Three bones in the middle ear—the hammer, the anvil, and the stirrup—act as levers to transmit the changes in pressure from the eardrum to the oval window of the inner ear.

[FIGURE 9]

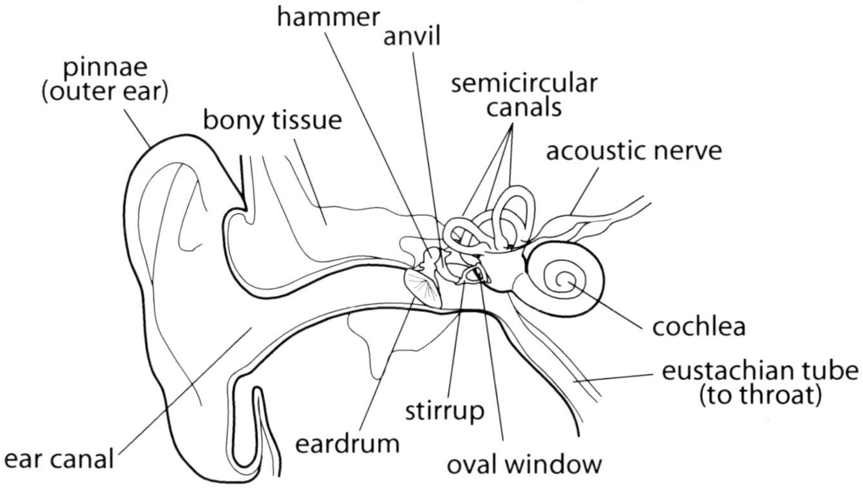

The diagram shows the human ear where sound is received and converted to nerve impulses that enable you to hear the sound.

The oval window is the membrane that covers the opening to the fluid-filled cochlea, a coiled, shell-like structure where the pressure impulses are changed to nerve impulses that travel to the brain. It is your brain that makes you aware of the pressure changes (sound) that reach your ear.

The inner ear also contains three semicircular canals. These tubes are filled with fluids and nerve endings that send impulses to your brain. On the basis of the impulses received from these canals, you are aware of your body's motion and position. In response to the signals received from the semicircular canals, your brain sends out impulses to your muscles that enable you to maintain your balance and know how you are oriented in space.

Most sounds do not consist of a single pulse but of many pulses closely spaced in time that are produced by a vibrating object. That vibrating object could be the string of a violin or cello, the head of a drum, the motor of a car, or, most commonly, the vocal cords of another person. Your most common means of communication is through spoken words, and it is the vibration of vocal cords that gives rise to the sounds we call speech.

In the next experiment, you will investigate another model to explain how sound, which usually consists of many air pulses closely spaced in time, travels through air.

2.3 Waves: A Model for Sound

Materials:
- long (about 3-4 inches when unstretched) steel Slinky or several short ones joined together by twist-ties
- long, smooth floor
- a partner
- small piece of yarn

We can feel pulses of air and we can hear sound, but we cannot see either sound or pulses of air. We need a model to show how air molecules pushed by a vibrating object can push other molecules and transmit a pressure pulse through air-filled space. We can visualize how this happens by sending pulses and multiple pulses along a Slinky.

If you do not have a long Slinky, use twist-ties to fasten several short Slinkies together. Place the Slinky on a long, smooth floor. Hold on to one end of the Slinky while a partner holds on to the other end. To produce what corresponds to a pressure pulse in air, ask your partner to hold his or her end of the Slinky firmly in place on the floor while you push your end of the Slinky forward (toward your partner) quickly and then pull it back. Watch the pulse as it travels along the Slinky to your partner. Does it reflect back toward you after it reaches your partner's fixed hand? Can sound be reflected?

As you know, sounds can move from you to a partner at the same time sounds from your partner are moving toward you—when you both talk at the same time! Can pulses on a Slinky pass through one another the way sounds do? To find out, have your partner generate a pulse in the same way you do and at the same time. Do the pulses pass through one another? Does the pulse you produce reach your partner? Does your partner's pulse reach you?

Your push on the Slinky corresponds to the push air molecules receive when a pulse of air is created by an object being struck, such as a drum or a bell. To create the multiple pulses that would be produced by a vibrating object that generates sound, you can repeatedly and rhythmically move the end of the Slinky forward and back while your partner holds the far end still. Watch the series of pulses move along the Slinky to the other end. When you stop producing pulses, watch the last few you generated. Are they reflected back toward you when they reach the opposite end?

Such a series of evenly spaced pulses makes up a longitudinal wave (see Figure 10). The regions where the coils of the spring (the Slinky) are close together are called compressions. They correspond to increased air pressure where molecules of air are pushed together by a vibrating object. The regions where the coils are more widely separated than normal are called rarefactions. They correspond to areas of reduced air pressure where the molecules are less concentrated than normal. A rarefaction forms when a vibrating object swings back after having pushed molecules together. As it swings back, there is a zone where the molecules are less concentrated because many of the molecules that would normally be there were pushed away to create a compression.

[FIGURE 10]

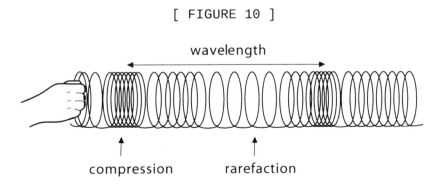

A longitudinal wave can be produced on a Slinky.

The wave is called longitudinal because it moves down the length of the Slinky. It is transmitted by the forward and backward movement of the coils that make up the Slinky. The distance between one compression and the next, or between one rarefaction and the next, is a wavelength. The number of waves generated per second is the frequency of the waves.

Longitudinal waves explain how sound travels from a source to your ears. The vibrating object that produces the sound compresses air molecules. That region of compression then pushes on molecules ahead of it until the wave of air compression reaches your ear. You can visualize the motion of such a wave by remembering how a longitudinal wave travels on a Slinky. Your hand corresponds to the vibrating object that produces the waves. The coils correspond to air molecules that are alternately compressed and rarefied.

Of course, the Slinky is only a one-dimensional model. In the three-dimensional world we live in, sound waves, unless blocked, spread out in all directions. We can think of the three-dimensional wave as a huge number of Slinkies carrying compressions and rarefactions outward from a single source of vibration.

It is important to realize that although longitudinal waves move along a Slinky or through the air, the coils of the Slinky or the molecules of air simply move back and forth. They carry the wave, but they do not move with it. You can demonstrate this by tying a piece of yarn to one coil of the Slinky. Does the yarn move along the Slinky or does it simply oscillate (swing) back and forth? Another example of such a wave is the kind that crowds do at a sports stadium. The fans all stay in the same place as the wave travels around the stadium.

Materials:

-long Slinky or several short ones joined together by twist-ties

-long, smooth floor

-2 partners

-small piece of yarn

In Experiment 2.3, you examined longitudinal waves and saw how they can be used to illustrate the way sound waves travel through air. You made longitudinal waves by moving the end of the Slinky forward and backward in a rhythmical manner with your hand. The distance between wave pulses was called the wavelength. But suppose you move the end of the Slinky quickly to the right and left on the floor instead of back and forth, while your partner holds the other end tightly in place (see Figure 11a). What do these waves look like?

The waves you generate by moving your hand right and left as you hold one end of a Slinky are called transverse waves. They are called transverse because they arise from a motion that is *across* the Slinky rather than *along* it.

The amplitude of a transverse wave is the amount the wave moves to either side of its normal position. The wavelength is the distance from one crest (or trough) to the next (see Figure 11b). Using the Slinky, how can you make waves with a large and a small amplitude? How can you make waves with a large wavelength? With a small wavelength? Estimate the amplitude and wavelength of a number of different waves made on the Slinky. It may be easier to do this if you ask a second person to hold your end of the Slinky. Then you can watch the waves from a position to one side of the middle of the Slinky.

Are transverse waves reflected when they reach the opposite end of the Slinky? Will transverse pulses or waves pass through one another?

Tie a small piece of yarn to the Slinky. Have one of your partners send transverse pulses down the Slinky. Does

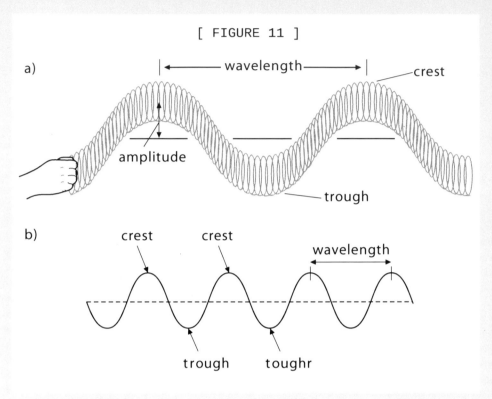

[FIGURE 11]

a) The same Slinky can be used to produce transverse
waves. b) Transverse waves have crests and troughs.
One wavelength is the distance from one crest
(or trough) to the next.

the yarn move with the wave or does it simply move back
and forth as the wave passes? How is the behavior of the
yarn similar to its behavior when you sent longitudinal
waves along the Slinky? How is it different?

Watch a stick floating on a lake or pond. As a water
wave passes the stick does the stick move along with the
wave or does it bob up and down and remain where it was?
Are water waves longitudinal or transverse?

Suppose your partners both generate a transverse pulse
of about the same size on the same side of the Slinky.
That is, one partner moves his hand to his right and back

again at the same time the second partner at the other end of the Slinky moves his hand to his left and back again (see Figure 12a). What do you predict will happen when the two pulses meet? Have them try it! Were you right? How can you explain what you observed?

Have your partners produce transverse pulses of about the same size on opposite sides of the Slinky, as shown in Figure 12b. Predict what will happen when these transverse pulses meet. You may want to observe this several times. Was your prediction correct?

How can a transverse wave be used to represent a longitudinal wave?

Standing Waves

Standing waves are waves that stay in place. They form when a reflected wave matches an incoming wave in frequency, wavelength, and amplitude. To produce a standing wave, have a partner hold one end of the long Slinky in place while you generate transverse waves. Produce the waves at such a rate that the frequency, wavelength, and amplitude remain constant

[FIGURE 12]

a)

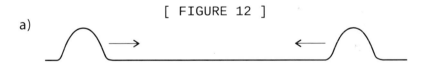

b)

a) Pulses are made on the same side of a Slinky. What will happen when the two pulses meet? b) Pulses are made on opposite sides of a Slinky. What will happen when the two pulses meet?

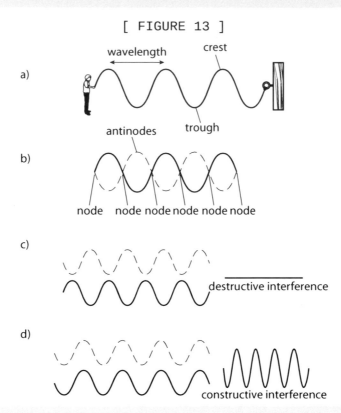

[FIGURE 13]

Standing waves can be produced when a reflected wave matches an incoming wave in frequency and amplitude (its size). a) A wave is sent into a fixed barrier where it is reflected. b) The incoming wave (solid wavy line) and the reflected wave (dotted wavy line) superimpose on one another. Points where the waves always cancel one another are called nodes. Between the nodes are antinodes where crests and troughs from the two waves alternately add or cancel. Notice that nodes are half a wavelength apart and so are antinodes. c) When crests from the reflected wave superimpose on troughs from the incoming wave, destructive interference occurs. In the case of a spring, the result is a perfectly straight spring. d) When crests and troughs from the reflected wave are superimposed on matching crests and troughs from the incoming wave, constructive interference occurs with maximum amplitude at the antinodes.

and overlap with the reflected waves. At a certain frequency you will find that there are one or more points on the Slinky that remain fixed in position—they do not move. These nonmoving points are called nodes (see Figure 13.) At the nodes, the waves you are generating and the reflected waves always cancel each other. At points midway between the nodes, you will find antinodes. Here the waves alternately come together to make waves twice as high as either wave alone or cancel completely so that there is no wave at all.

The overlapping (superposition) of one wave on another is called interference. When the amplitude of the waves is twice as large as the waves you are generating, we say the waves are interfering with one another constructively. When the wave crests are on opposite sides of the Slinky and cancel each other, we say the waves are interfering destructively.

Can you produce longitudinal standing waves on your Slinky?

EXPLORING ON YOUR OWN

Show that the velocity at which either longitudinal or transverse waves travel is equal to the product of their wavelength and their frequency:

$$velocity = wavelength \times frequency$$

2.5 Sound Waves and a Horn

Materials:
- bugle or a similar wind instrument
- a partner
- bubble-making solution
- shallow dish
- large room

You have seen that a wave can transmit energy, but not matter. When you launch a longitudinal wave on a Slinky, the coils move back and forth about a central position. They do not move along the Slinky with the wave. We have used the Slinky as a model for sound waves. Therefore, it is reasonable to believe that while sound waves travel outward from a source, the air itself simply oscillates (swings) about a central position like the coils of a Slinky.

A bugle or a similar instrument will demonstrate that the air that transmits sound does not move with the sound waves. If you can play a bugle or another wind instrument, you can demonstrate this principle for yourself. If you do not play such an instrument, ask a partner to help you.

Pour bubble-making solution into a shallow dish. Then dip the wide end of the horn into the solution and blow a few notes on the instrument. Watch the bubble at the end of the horn. Can you or a partner hear sound on the opposite side of the room? Does the air in the bubble at the end of the horn move to the opposite side of the room, or does it remain in the bubble? How is this experiment with sound similar to what you saw with the Slinky in Experiment 2.3? How is it different?

Materials:

- Styrofoam or paper cup
- string
- tape
- chair or small table
- several sheets of paper or wrapping paper
- small nail
- fine sand or water with food coloring
- ruler
- stopwatch

Transverse waves, explored in Experiment 2.4, are useful for analyzing many kinds of motion. Even motions that do not appear to be wavelike can be changed to transverse waves. The waves can then be used to analyze the motion.

To see how a swinging pendulum can be transformed into a transverse wave, make a sturdy pendulum from a Styrofoam or paper cup and string, as shown in Figure 14.

The pendulum is suspended from the side of a chair or small table over a floor. It should be suspended from two points to ensure that it will swing along a straight line and not wobble. You will need a long sheet of paper from a roll or one made by joining several smaller sheets. Use a nail to punch a small hole in the bottom of the cup and cover it from outside the cup with tape. Center one end of the long sheet of paper under the pendulum. Fill the pendulum with fine sand or water to which food coloring has been added. Remove the tape, pull the pendulum a short distance to one side and release it. Then pull the paper slowly at a steady rate beneath and perpendicular to

[FIGURE 14]

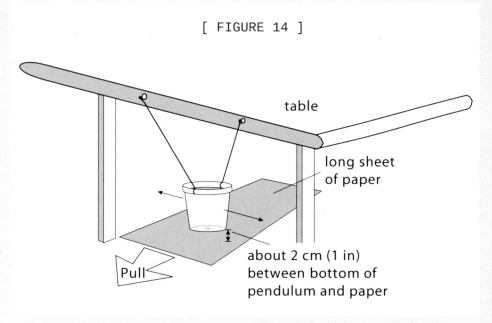

table

long sheet
of paper

about 2 cm (1 in)
between bottom of
pendulum and paper

Pull

What pattern is made on a moving sheet of paper by a pendulum that swings above the paper?

the motion of the swinging pendulum so that the contents of the cup fall slowly onto the moving paper. Continue to pull the paper until the other end lies beneath the pendulum. Then stop the pendulum, cover the hole in the bottom, and empty any remaining sand or liquid into an appropriate container.

Now look at the pattern the swinging pendulum made on the paper. What is it? How can you use the pattern's amplitude to determine the distance the pendulum swung to either side of its rest position? How can you use the pattern to determine when the speed of the pendulum was zero? How can you determine when its speed was greatest?

How can you change the amplitude of the waves you see on the paper? How can you change the wavelength of the waves you see on the paper?

Using a stopwatch, how can you determine the frequency of the pendulum from the pattern on the paper?

EXPLORING ON YOUR OWN

What other kinds of motion can be converted to transverse waves? Design ways to convert these motions into transverse waves that can be recorded.

What kind of pattern will be made by a point on the rim of a wheel that is spinning in place? What kind of pattern will be made by a point on the rim of a rolling wheel? Figure out ways to record these patterns on paper or cardboard.

What is simple harmonic motion? How is it related to a transverse wave?

More About Waves

You have seen that longitudinal waves can explain how sound moves from a vibrating source through air. The vibrating object or objects, which could be someone's vocal cords, produce longitudinal waves by forming compressions and rarefactions in the air. By successive collisions of air molecules, the sound wave is carried outward through the space around the source. The intensity (loudness) of the sound becomes smaller as it spreads outward. You have evidence from Experiment 1.7 that this is true. The farther you are from someone, the harder it is to hear what that person is saying. As sound energy spreads away from its source, the quantity of energy passing through an area becomes smaller. The same is true of any form of energy carried by waves, such as light, radio or television signals, and X rays.

The longitudinal waves you made on a Slinky were one-dimensional; they moved along a line. In this chapter, you will find it is possible to make transverse waves on a rope that travels in all three dimensions of space. You will also find that you can observe transverse water waves traveling over a surface. Water waves provide a model for many properties common to all types of waves.

Materials:
- long jump rope or heavy cloth clothesline
- post or some other fixed object
- an adult or a strong friend

In Chapter 2, you produced standing waves on a Slinky. Standing waves are waves that stay in place. They form when a reflected wave matches an incoming wave in frequency, wavelength, and amplitude. You can also generate standing waves on a rope. To do so, tie one end of a long jump rope or heavy cloth clothesline to a post or some other fixed object. A long rope (3 m [10 ft] or more) is best. Try generating standing waves by holding the free end of the rope and moving your hand up and down to send vertical waves. You can make standing waves that are such that the distance between you and the opposite end of the rope are equal to $1/2$ wavelength, 1 wavelength, $1 1/2$ wavelengths, and so on.

The easiest standing wave to make is one where the wavelength is twice the distance between you and the other fixed end. Both your hand and the fixed end of the rope will be nodes, as shown in Figure 15a. (Of course, your hand has to move a little in order to overcome friction and keep the wave going.)

Once you have established that first standing wave, try to produce some others, such as those shown in Figure 15b. They will be more difficult to generate, but keep trying. You may want to ask an adult or a strong friend to help you.

You can also produce three-dimensional transverse standing waves on a rope. The simplest is again one where the end nodes are half a wavelength apart. This is the standing wave you produce when someone is jumping rope (see Figures 16ai and 16aii). If the distance between

[FIGURE 15]

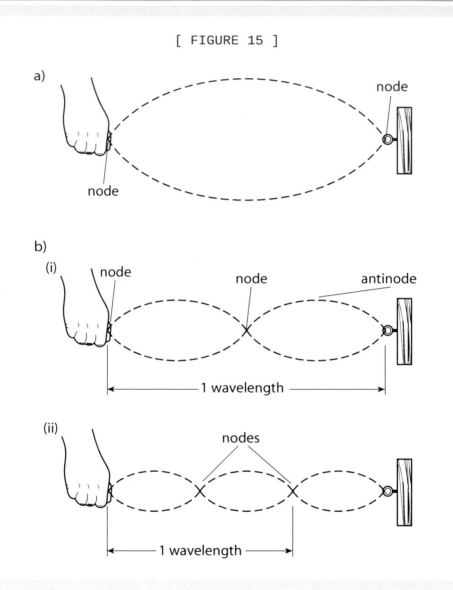

Standing waves can be generated on a rope. a) A standing wave with only two nodes that are $^1/_2$ wavelength
apart. b)(i) A standing wave with three nodes. The
distance between the two end nodes is one wavelength.
(ii) A standing wave with four nodes. The distance
between the two end nodes is 1.5 wavelengths.

[FIGURE 16]

a)

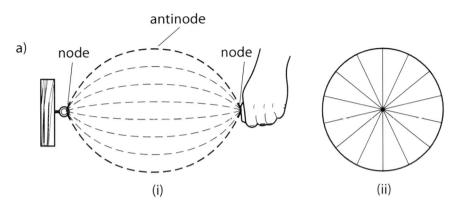

(i)   (ii)

b)

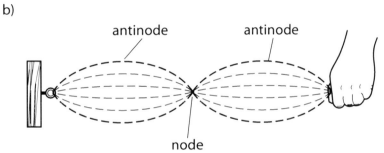

c)

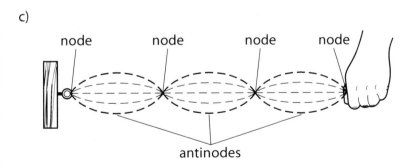

Three-dimensional standing waves on a rope. a(i) Two nodes, one antinode. a(ii) The view from the end of the rope. b) Three nodes, two antinodes. c) Four nodes, three antinodes.

you and the fixed end of the rope is 3 m (about 10 ft), what is the wavelength of the wave? Remember, the nodes in a standing wave are half a wavelength apart.

If you turn the rope twice as fast (double the frequency and halve the wavelength), you can produce a node in the center of the rope as well as the nodes at each end, as shown in Figure 16b. How many antinodes do you see? If you are still 3 m from the fixed end of the rope, what is the wavelength now? Can you turn the rope fast enough to produce a total of 4 nodes (Figure 16c)? How many antinodes do you see?

EXPLORING ON YOUR OWN

You can set up standing sound waves that have a lovely tone. Moisten your finger and rub it around the rim of an empty wine glass while you hold the base of the glass firmly against a table. What happens to the sound when you add water to the glass? Where else do you find sounds that result from standing waves?

Investigate the many useful applications of ultrasonics.

Materials:

- ripple tank, or a large, clear plastic pan or box, such as a large glass baking dish that has a smooth flat bottom, a clear plastic sweater box from a variety store, or a large, clear acrylic box picture frame, at least 11 in x 14 in
- 2 chairs or tables
- ceiling light or a lamp
- clear bulb with a straight-line filament (optional)
- water
- ruler
- strips of paper
- large sheet of white paper
- strips of soft cloth
- 12 flat blocks of wood about 15 cm (6 in) wide and 5–10 cm (2–4 in) tall
- wooden dowel (or a wax candle)
- stiff piece of wire (one cut from a coat hanger works well)
- length of rubber tubing or old garden hose
- glass plates about 10 cm (4 in) on a side, or a clear, water-filled, plastic sandwich box and cover
- cardboard
- pencil

The best way to look at the behavior of water waves is to use a ripple tank. Your school's science department may have one you can borrow. If not, you can use a large, clear plastic pan or box or a large glass baking dish that has a smooth, flat bottom. A clear plastic sweater box will also serve the purpose. So will a large, clear acrylic box picture frame that is at least 11 in x 14 in. It can be obtained from a variety store. You may even have one in your home that holds a large photograph. Ask permission before using items in your home.

Support the clear container, which we will call a water tank, on two chairs or tables with a light directly over the pan, as shown in Figure 17a. A clear bulb with a straight-line filament turned so that its end acts as a point of light shining on the water tank works best, but an ordinary frosted bulb will do. Pour water into the tank to a depth of about 2 cm (1 in). Be sure the water tank is level so that the water is the same depth everywhere. Strips of paper placed under one end of the tank can be used to level it if necessary. Spread a large sheet of white paper on the floor beneath the tank.

Tap the outside of your water tank gently on the side at a steady rate. Look at the pattern on the white paper beneath the tank. Can you make a standing wave pattern, one in which the waves do not appear to move?

Dip your finger into the center of the water. Look at the wave pulse you can see on the white paper. What shape does the pulse have? How does it move? What happens when the pulse reaches the walls of the tank? To reduce unwanted reflected waves, cover the inside surfaces of the water tank's walls with strips of soft cloth.

Reflecting Waves
Stand a flat piece of wood about 15 cm (6 in) wide and 5–10 cm (2–4 in) tall upright in the water, as shown in Figure 17b. Again, use your finger to generate a wave pulse some distance from the wood barrier. Watch the wave's image on the white-paper screen to see what happens when the wave pulse hits the flat wooden surface. If the wood represents a mirror and your finger a source of light, where does the image appear to be? If the wood represents a large wall and your finger a source of sound, where does the echo appear to originate?

[FIGURE 17]

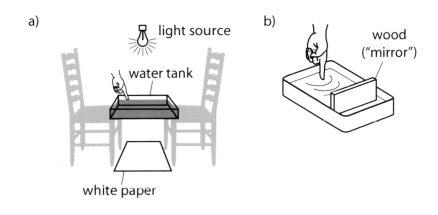

a)

light source

water tank

white paper

b)

wood ("mirror")

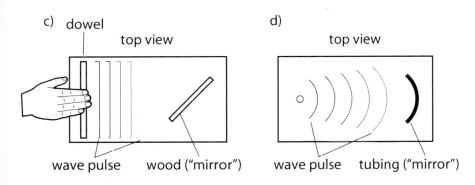

c) dowel

top view

wave pulse   wood ("mirror")

d)

top view

wave pulse   tubing ("mirror")

a) A water tank rests on two chairs. It is illuminated by a light above the tank. Waves can be seen on the white paper screen on the floor beneath the tank. b) A piece of wood can serve as a reflecting surface or "mirror." c) Placing the "mirror" at an angle to the waves will allow you to see how the angles that the incoming (incident) waves make with the mirror compare with those made by the reflected waves. d) A curved piece of rubber tubing can serve as a concave reflector or "mirror."

To see how the waves reflect with regard to angle, use a piece of wooden dowel (or a wax candle) with a diameter greater than the water's depth to generate a straight wave front, as shown in Figure 17c. If you touch the dowel with your fingertips and pull it toward you a short distance, you can generate a very clear wave front. Set the wooden "mirror" so that the wave strikes it at different angles. How does the angle at which the waves strike the flat surface compare with the angle at which they are reflected?

A Concave Reflector

You have probably seen concave-shaped "dishes" along the sidelines at televised football games. They are used to focus sound waves from the field. To see how this works with waves, make a curved reflector for your water tank. Find a length of rubber tubing or old garden hose that is about as long as the width of your water tank. Put a stiff piece of wire (one cut from a coat hanger works well) inside the tube. Bend the tubing to make a concave surface (the wire will maintain the curvature) and place it near one end of the tank, as shown in Figure 17d.

At the opposite end of the tank, dip your finger into the water to create a wave pulse. What happens to the wave when it reaches the concave reflector? Watch the image of the wave on the white-paper screen carefully. You will see that the wave comes together at a point in front of the concave reflector. This point is where the image would form if the wave were a light wave. If the waves were sound waves, what would you want to put there in order to hear better?

Now, dip your finger into the water repeatedly at a steady rate to send a series of waves toward the concave reflector. Do these waves also converge at a point in front of the reflector?

Next, generate a series of equally spaced waves by moving the wooden dowel or candle in rhythmic fashion. Do these waves converge to a point in front of the concave surface?

Now reverse the process. Dip your finger into the tank at the point where the waves converged. Can you see on the white paper a reflected pulse coming from the reflector? Make a series of waves by dipping your finger into the water repeatedly at a steady rate to send a series of waves toward the concave reflector. Can you see a "beam" of parallel waves coming from the reflector? If the waves were light waves, you would have a spotlight and a beam such as the kind you see coming from a lighthouse. What would you have if the waves were sound waves?

Refracted Waves

As you probably know, light waves are refracted (bent) when they are seen passing through water and then through air. You can demonstrate this by placing a pencil in a glass of water and looking at it from the side. This bending of light happens because the light waves slow down when they pass from air to water or glass. Refraction accounts for the way a lens is able to bring sunlight together to form a bright spot that is hot enough to start a campfire, as any Boy or Girl Scout will tell you. Because light of different colors is refracted differently, white light is broken up into a spectrum when it passes through a glass or plastic prism.

As you will find in Chapter 4, sound waves can also be refracted when they pass from air into a different gas. To see how waves refract in your water tank, you will need a stack of 2 or 3 glass plates about 10 cm (4 in) on a side, or a clear plastic sandwich box. Place the glass plates or sandwich box (upside down) near the center of the water tank. Add enough water to make a region of very shallow water over the plates or box, as shown in Figure 18a. The shallow water represents a different medium than the deep water. If the deep water represents air, the shallow water could represent glass or water.

Next, use the wooden dowel to make a wave pulse. Watch the pulse as it passes from deep to shallow water. You will see the wave's speed decrease as it enters the shallow water. Now turn the plates so that the wave enters the shallow water at an angle. Stand a piece of cardboard upright on each side of the plates, as shown in Figure 18b, so that the part of the wave that does not enter the shallow water is reflected away. What happens to the direction the straight wave is traveling when it enters the shallow water?

Repeat the experiment, but this time move the dowel in rhythmic fashion to produce a series of waves. What happens to these waves as they pass from deep to shallow

[FIGURE 18]

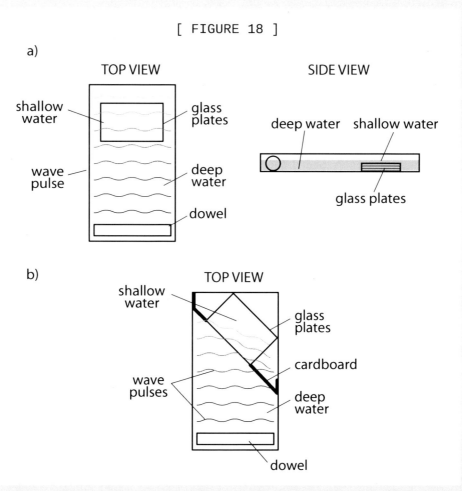

Water waves refract (bend) when they travel from deep water to shallow water.

water? If you could make lens-shaped (oval) plates, what would the pattern of the waves look like as they passed from deep to shallow and back to deep water?

Diffraction

You have probably looked at objects through a microscope. The lenses in the microscope magnify objects so that things as small as bacteria (0.001–0.005 mm) can be seen. However, you may not know that there is a limit to what can be seen under a microscope. Objects with diameters of 0.0001 mm cannot be seen through an ordinary microscope. Light waves simply bend around such small objects instead of being reflected back by them. We say the light diffracts around the objects. The same thing happens when light waves pass through very narrow openings. They diffract around the edges of the opening.

You can see waves diffract in your water tank. Have a friend hold a pencil upright in the middle of the tank. Then generate a series of waves with your fingertip at one end of the tank, as shown in Figure 19a. As you can see, the waves pass around the pencil. Someone who could see

[FIGURE 19]

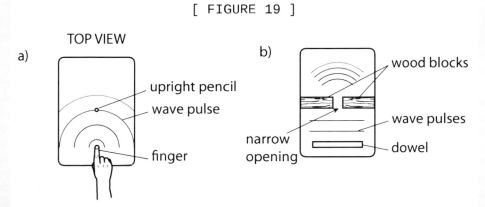

a) A pencil casts no "shadow" because waves diffract around it. b) What happens when waves pass through a narrow opening?

only the waves that reach the other end of the tank would not be aware of the pencil. It casts no "shadow"; that is, the waves are not blocked and reflected as they are by larger objects.

Replace the pencil with a much larger object, such as the wooden block you used before. Again, generate waves with your fingertip. Can you see the "shadow" cast by the block? Is there any diffraction of waves around the block?

Next, stand two blocks of wood upright near the center of your tank. Use the blocks to form a narrow opening, as shown in Figure 19b. Generate a series of waves with your fingertip and then with the wooden dowel. What happens to the waves as they pass through the narrow opening?

Do you think sound waves diffract? What evidence do you have to support your answer?

EXPLORING ON YOUR OWN

Place a cup of coffee, tea, or water beneath a lightbulb so that you can see the liquid's surface better. Can you establish standing waves on the water surface by tapping on the side of the cup? Can you establish standing waves in the cup by placing it on a vibrating object such as a refrigerator that is running?

Interference occurs when the crest from one wave source constantly falls on the trough of another and vice versa. The two waves cancel, producing a node. Where crests fall on crests or troughs on troughs, there are antinodes where the light is brighter. You can see the interference pattern established by light by looking at a fluorescent tube through a diffraction grating. See if you can demonstrate interference using sound waves.

PROPERTIES OF SOUND

You have seen how sounds are made by vibrating objects and how longitudinal waves can be used to explain the way sound is transmitted through air. In this chapter you can measure the speed of sound in air and carry out experiments to see whether sound can be transmitted by solids and liquids. You will also have an opportunity to look for the wave properties of sound. Can the properties of waves that you examined in Experiment 3.2—reflection, refraction, and diffraction—be found with sound?

4.1 Transmission of Sound

Materials:

- watch or clock that makes a soft ticking sound
- wooden ruler
- wooden table
- metal tabletop, metal pipe, or metal doorknob
- dining fork
- heavy string
- swimming area
- 2 stones
- 2 small, flat stones
- plastic bucket
- water

You know that sound can be transmitted through air by longitudinal sound waves made by alternating regions of compression and rarefaction. These waves, but not the air that carries them, move from the vibrating source of sound to your ears. You know, too, that sound cannot travel through a vacuum. But can it travel through other media?

If you replace the air in an enclosed space with other gases, such as hydrogen, helium, and carbon dioxide, you can show that all gases transmit sound. But can sound travel through solids and liquids?

To see whether or not sound can be transmitted through a solid, hold one end of a wooden ruler next to your ear. Scratch the far end of the ruler with your fingernail. Keep your finger at the same place, but turn the ruler around so that it is directed away from your ear. Scratch the ruler again.

In the first case, wood carried sound from the source to your ear. In the second case, the source of sound was the same distance from your ear but only air lay between your ear and the source of the sound. Which is the better transmitter of sound, wood or air? What makes you think so?

To further test sound transmission by a solid, hold a ticking watch next to your ear. Then move it an arm's length away. How well can you hear it now? Next, place the watch on a wooden tabletop. Place your ear on the tabletop an arm's length away from the watch. How well can you hear the watch now? Does wood conduct sound? Does it conduct sound as well as air?

If possible, repeat the experiment on a metal tabletop. If such a surface is not available, use a metal pipe, or hold the watch against a doorknob while you place your ear against the metal knob on the other side of the door. Can sound be transmitted through metal?

Hang a dining fork on a long piece of heavy string. Let the fork strike against the edge of a table and listen to the sound it makes. Repeat the experiment after you put the end of the string in your ear and hold it there with your index finger, as shown in Figure 20. Does sound

[FIGURE 20]

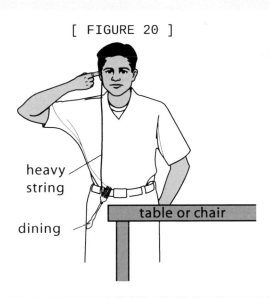

Is sound transmitted better by air or by string?

travel better in the solid string or in air? Can you detect tones through the string that you did not hear through the air? Where have you heard such sounds before?

Remove the string from the dining fork and pluck the tines of the fork. Can you hear the sound if you place the tines near your ear? Repeat the experiment, but this time put the handle of the fork between your teeth after you pluck the tines. Does sound travel better through bone or through air?

If you have access to a swimming area and have **an adult** with you, have someone bang two stones together underwater while you listen with your head submerged. Repeat the experiment in air with the stones separated by the same distance from your ears. Can sound be transmitted through water?

If you cannot do this experiment in a swimming area, you can do something similar with two small, flat stones and a plastic bucket filled with water. Hold one ear against the outside of the bucket while someone rubs two small, flat stones together underwater on the opposite side of the bucket. Can you hear the sound made by the stones? Can you hear it better through water or through air?

EXPLORING ON YOUR OWN

Build a set of "telephones" from two plastic-coated paper coffee cups, a long piece of monofilament fishing line, and paper clips. Punch small holes in the bottoms of the cups, and thread the ends of the line through the holes. Tie the ends of the line to paper clips so they will stay inside the cups. Use a cup as both transmitter and receiver to talk to a friend who holds the other cup. Be sure that you talk softly so that you cannot hear each other through sound transmitted by air. What is the range of your telephone? What other materials can you use to make "telephone lines?"

Materials:

- a space large enough so that you can see someone at least 500 m or 500 yds away
- long measuring tape
- a friend
- board and a hammer, cymbals, or another device that will make a loud sound
- stopwatch
- notebook
- pocket calculator (optional)
- building with a large flat surface that will reflect the sound
- 2 flat boards

If you have ever sat in the bleachers at a baseball game, you have probably noticed that you hear the crack of bat against the ball *after* you see the baseball leave the bat. This tells you that the speed of light in air is greater than the speed of sound in the same medium. This is not surprising in view of the fact that nothing moves faster than the speed of light, which is 300,000,000 meters (984,000,000 feet) per second.

An Approximation of the Speed of Sound
You can make a rough determination of the speed of sound by making use of the fact that light travels much faster than sound. You will need to find a place where you can see a friend who is at least 500 m or 500 yds (five football fields) away. The distance between you and your friend can be measured by repeatedly using a long measuring tape, or you can pace it off once you measure

the length of your pace. The friend will make a loud sound by striking a board with a hammer, slamming cymbals together, or making a sound in some similar way so that you can see when the sound is made. The moment you *see* the sound being made, start a stopwatch. Stop the watch as soon as you *hear* the sound. Record the time in a notebook.

Repeat the experiment several times and find the average time for the sound to reach you. Divide the distance between you and the place where the sound was made by the time for the sound to reach you. On the basis of the data you collected, what is the speed of sound?

A More Accurate Determination of the Speed of Sound
As you know, an echo is a reflected sound. You can use an echo to determine the speed of sound. First, find a building with a large flat surface that will reflect the sound you make by clapping two flat boards together. Stand about 50 m or 50 yds from the building and be sure you can hear the echo clearly. The time between making the clap and hearing the echo is much too short to time accurately. However, you can duplicate the method that Sir Isaac Newton used to make an accurate measurement of sound's velocity.

What you need to do is adjust the rate at which you clap the two boards together so that each clap is made at the same time you hear the echo from the previous clap. The time between claps then will be the time for the sound to travel from you to the building and back again, or the time for sound to travel about 100 m or 100 yds. Once you have learned to clap the boards together at that rate, continue clapping for about 40 or more claps while a partner uses a stopwatch to record the time to make a specific number of claps. Be sure your partner calls the clap at which he or she starts timing as clap number zero. Why should it be zero and not one?

What was the total number of claps? How long did it take to make those claps? What do you determine the speed of sound to be? Suppose you were 50 m from the building that reflected the sounds and you made 40 claps in 13.2 seconds. The time between claps was then:

$$\frac{13.2 \text{ s}}{40} = 0.33 \text{ s}$$

The sound then, on the average, traveled 100 m in 0.33 s. The speed of sound according to this data is:

$$\frac{100 \text{ m}}{0.33 \text{ s}} = 300 \text{ m/s}$$

What is the speed of sound according to your data?

Use the same technique to measure the speed of sound at different temperatures. To do this you will have to measure the speed of sound during different seasons of the year. What do your results reveal? Does sound travel faster in summer than in winter? If it does, can you explain why it might do so?

EXPLORING ON YOUR OWN

Design and carry out experiments to see if sound is affected by weather.

Now that you know the speed of sound, how can you use it to determine distance?

Just by listening to a band or orchestra when it starts to play, what evidence do you have that all wavelengths of sound travel at the same speed?

How do bats use sound to fly at night and locate food?

How do dolphins use sound to locate and distinguish objects in their environment?

4.3 The Speed of Sound in Another Medium

You have found the speed of sound in air, but from Experiment 4.1, you know that sound can be transmitted by solids and liquids as well as by gases. In this experiment you can compare the speed of sound in a solid medium to its speed in air. To do so, you will need a long sidewalk or a metal fence or railing at least 50 m long.

Place your ear against one end of the length of sidewalk or fence. Have your partner strike the other end with a hammer. The sound will travel through the solid and through the air. But the sounds transmitted by the two media will have different tones. Listen carefully! If the two sounds reach you at the same time, the sound must travel through the two media with the same speed. If one transmits sound faster than the other, you should be able to detect a short time lapse between the two sounds. If you cannot detect any time delay, try increasing the distance between you and the person sending the sound.

Which sound reaches you first, the one carried by air or the one carried by the solid? Or do they arrive simultaneously even if the distance between you and the source of the sound is large? Based on your observations, is the speed of sound greater in air or in the solid you tested?

Sound can be transmitted by all gases; however, the speed of sound in these gases is not the same as it is in ordinary air. Table 1 shows the speed of sound in several different gases. Carefully examine all the data in the table.

As you can see from Table 1, the speed of sound is very different for different media. Based on the data in the table and your own measurements of the speed of sound

Table 1: The speed of sound, measured in meters per second (m/s) and feet per second (ft/s), in different substances. All measurements were made at 20°C (68°F) unless otherwise indicated.

SUBSTANCE	SPEED (m/s)	SPEED (ft/s)
GASES		
carbon dioxide (at 0°C)	260	853
carbon dioxide	268	879
helium	923	3,027
hydrogen (at 0°C)	1,290	4,230
hydrogen	1,315	4,313
LIQUIDS		
alcohol (ethyl)	1,210	3,969
mercury	1,450	4,756
water	1,469	4,818
SOLIDS		
lead	1,230	4,034
brass	3,505	11,496
granite	3,950	12,956
aluminum	5,100	16,728
iron	5,120	16,794

in air, what can you conclude about the speed of sound in solids and liquids as compared with gases? What effect does temperature have on the speed of sound in gases? How is the speed of sound in a gas affected by the gas's density (its mass per volume)? Is the same true for solids?

EXPLORING ON YOUR OWN

How can you use your measurement of the speed of sound to determine the distance between you and the lightning triggered by a thunderstorm? Remember, thunder is caused by the expansion of air produced by the heating effects of lightning.

Does temperature have any effect on the speed of sound in a solid or liquid? If it does, what is it?

What factors determine the speed at which sound travels in a medium?

Design and carry out an experiment to measure the speed of light. This is a very challenging task. Bear in mind that the speed of light is the greatest speed known. You will need to either send the light over a very long path or measure very short time intervals or do both.

4.4 A Sounding Board

Materials:

-comb that has both heavy, widely spaced teeth and fine, closely spaced teeth

-hollow door

-tuning fork

-wooden table

Find a comb that has both heavy, widely spaced teeth and fine, closely spaced ones. Pull the end of your finger along the end of both types of teeth. Do the sounds produced by the two different types of teeth differ? If they do, can you explain why?

Repeat the experiment, but this time hold the edge of the comb opposite the teeth against the center of a hollow door. Why is the sound so much louder? In addition to the comb, what else is vibrating when you hold the comb against the door?

Strike a tuning fork against the heel of your shoe. Hold it in the air for a couple of seconds to get a sense of the loudness of the sound. Then hold the base of the tuning fork against a wooden tabletop. What happens to the loudness when the tuning fork is in contact with the table? Can you explain why?

EXPLORING ON YOUR OWN

What is an anechoic chamber? Where can you find one?

Materials:

- 2 long (about 60 cm or 2 ft) cardboard tubes such as mailing tubes
- object that produces a sound of low intensity, such as a wristwatch
- a friend
- smooth concrete wall in a quiet area

As you may know, when light reflects from a mirror or any smooth surface, the angle of reflection always equals the angle of incidence. As you can see from Figure 21a, the angle of incidence is the angle between a line perpendicular to the mirror at the point where an incoming light ray strikes the mirror and the light ray itself. The angle of reflection is the angle between that same perpendicular and the light ray after it has been reflected by the mirror. You can check on this for yourself by doing an experiment like the one shown in Figure 21b in an otherwise dark room.

To see if sound is reflected in the same way as light, you will need two long cardboard tubes, such as mailing tubes. You will also need an object that produces a sound of low intensity, such as a wristwatch, and a friend to help you. Your friend holds the watch at one end of a tube and holds the other end of that tube near a smooth concrete wall in a quiet area such as a basement or empty classroom. You hold the second tube. Have your friend turn the tube so that it makes an angle with the wall, as shown in Figure 22.

Hold your ear against one end of the second tube and place the other end near the end of the tube that your friend is holding. Slowly change the angle that your tube makes with the wall until you hear the faint sound most clearly and loudly. At that point, compare the angle that each tube makes with the wall.

Have your friend change the angle that his tube makes with the wall and repeat the experiment several times. After each

[FIGURE 21]

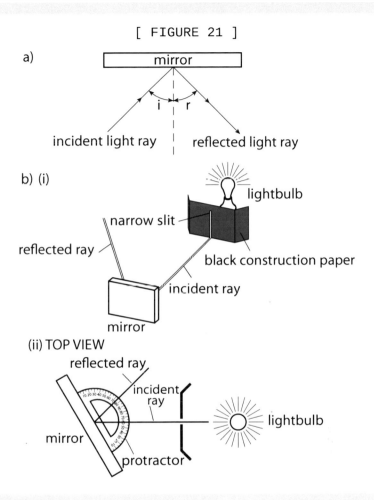

a) For light, angle i (the angle of incidence) always equals angle r (the angle of reflection). b) (i) View of an experiment designed to see if angle i equals angle r when light is reflected. (ii) Top view of experiment.

trial compare the angles the two tubes make with the wall. What can you conclude about the reflection of sound? Does reflected sound seem to follow the same law as reflected light?

Hold the spout (the narrow end) of a large metal or plastic funnel next to your ear. If you cannot find a funnel, roll several sheets of paper into a cone open at

[FIGURE 22]

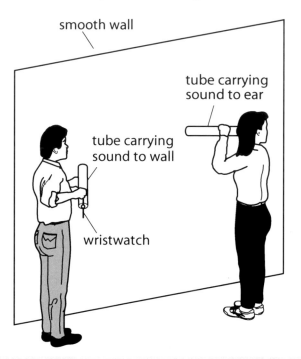

smooth wall

tube carrying
sound to ear

tube carrying
sound to wall

wristwatch

Do sound waves reflect in the same way that light does?

both ends. Place the narrow end of the cone next to your
ear. Turn the funnel or cone toward a source of sound.
What happens to the intensity (loudness) of the sound?
What happens when you remove the funnel? Explain why the
intensity of sound changes.

EXPLORING ON YOUR OWN

Explain how a megaphone works. See if you can design
one that carries sound better.

Before hearing aids were invented, people who were
hearing-impaired often used ear trumpets. What were ear
trumpets and how did they help people hear better?

Materials:
- seltzer tablets
- bottle or flask
- graduated cylinder or measuring cup
- water
- medium-size balloon
- twist-tie
- a friend
- ticking watch, clock, or a similar device that makes a soft sound
- meterstick or yardstick

In Experiment 3.2 you saw how water waves are bent (refracted) when they pass from deep water into shallow water. A similar thing happens when light passes from air to water or glass. A convex lens (magnifying glass) refracts sunlight so that the sun's nearly parallel rays can be focused (brought together) to form a small, bright, hot dot at the focal point of the lens.

To see if sound waves can be refracted, you can make a crude lens by filling a balloon with carbon dioxide. Experiments show that sound travels more slowly in carbon dioxide than it does in air (see Table 1). Based on what you saw in Experiment 3.2, as well as the fact that light travels more slowly in glass than in air, you would expect a carbon dioxide lens to converge sound waves to a focal point.

You can prepare carbon dioxide by dropping 4 or 5 broken seltzer tablets into a bottle or flask that holds about 50 mL (2 oz) of water. Once the tablets start fizzing, stretch a medium-size balloon a few times and then slip the neck of the balloon over the mouth of the flask, as shown in Figure 23a. Collect as much gas as

[FIGURE 23]

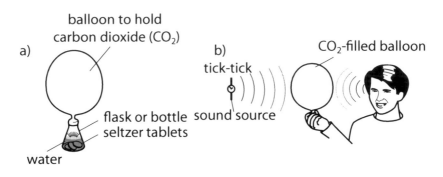

a) Adding seltzer tablets to water can be used to fill a balloon with carbon dioxide gas. b) A carbon dioxide lens can be used to focus sound waves.

possible. Then carefully remove the carbon dioxide-filled balloon and tie off its neck with a twist-tie.

Have a friend hold a ticking watch, clock, or a similar device that makes a soft sound near your ear. Then have your friend move the sound away from your ear until you can barely hear it. Now hold the carbon dioxide-filled balloon next to your ear, as shown in Figure 23b. Move the balloon back and forth between the source of the soft sound and your ear until the sound is loudest. What is the approximate focal length of your carbon dioxide lens? What would happen if you filled the balloon with helium or hydrogen? (See Table 1 following Experiment 4.3.)

EXPLORING ON YOUR OWN

Investigate some possible practical uses of the refraction of sound waves.

On a lake, sounds from a distant source that cannot be heard in the daytime can often be heard at night. Explain why.

Materials:

- a friend
- a hallway outside a room with a door
- tuning fork
- long table
- battery operated electronic buzzer (optional)

As you saw in Experiment 3.2, water waves will diffract around objects comparable in size or smaller than the wavelength. Water waves will also diffract when they pass through an opening comparable in size or smaller than the wavelength.

To see if sound waves diffract, have someone stand in a hallway outside a room with an open door. Stand in the doorway as the other person starts to talk to you. Then move into the room and stand to one side of the doorway rather than in it. Can you still hear the person? Are some sounds easier to hear than others?

Do sound waves diffract as they pass through the doorway? What evidence do you have to support your answer?

The experiment with a voice is rather crude, because a person's voice contains a great variety of wavelengths. You can test for diffraction with sound waves of constant wavelength or frequency. A middle-C tuning fork, which vibrates at 256 Hertz, or Hz (vibrations per second), will produce sounds with a wavelength of about 1.3 m. (Perhaps a music or science teacher or band director will let you use a tuning fork.) Since the frequency is usually written on the tuning fork, you can easily determine the wavelength of the sound, using your data from Experiment 4.2. Bear in mind that the speed of sound is equal to wavelength × frequency:

$$\text{speed} = \text{wavelength} \times \text{frequency, or } v = wf$$

Have someone hold the vibrating tuning fork at one end of a long table, while you stand at the opposite end. Turn your ear toward the sound, as shown in Figure 24. Lower your

[FIGURE 24]

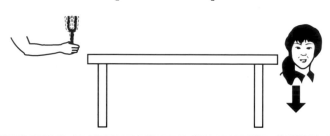

Do sound waves diffract around the edges of a table?
Does diffraction depend on the wavelength of the sound?

ear until it is well below the edge of the table. If the
sound waves diffract, there will be little change in the
loudness of the sound as you lower your head. If there is
minimal diffraction, you will note a distinct decrease in
loudness as your ear moves beneath the level of the table.
What do you find? What can you conclude?

If possible, repeat the experiment with a battery
operated electronic buzzer that produces a high-pitched sound
(3,000 Hz or higher). You can probably buy such a device at
an electronics store if your school does not have one you can
borrow. What wavelength of sound will the buzzer generate? Do
you detect a decrease in the loudness of the sound when your
ear is below the tabletop? Do you find any evidence that
diffraction is related to the wavelength of sound?

EXPLORING ON YOUR OWN

When cars with open windows pass by, why are you more
likely to hear bass notes from these car radios than
sounds of higher pitch?

The low-pitched sounds made by large whales in the
ocean can be detected hundreds of miles away, whereas
the higher-pitched sounds made by smaller whales
(dolphins) have a much shorter range. Explain why.

Why are foghorns made to produce low-pitched sounds?

Materials:

-car and driver

-tape

-9-volt buzzer

-plastic pail

-light rope

-a friend

-water tank used in Experiment 3.2

Have you ever listened to the sound of a train's whistle or an automobile's horn as it ap-proached you and then moved away from you? You may have noticed that the pitch of the sound is higher as it approaches you and lower as it moves away from you.

Ask a parent or another adult to drive by you in a car. Ask them to sound the car's horn as they approach you and continue to sound the horn after they have moved past you. Ask them to repeat the experiment several times with the car moving at different speeds.

How does the pitch of the sound change as the car moves past you? How are the sounds you hear affected by the car's speed?

To examine this effect in a more controlled way, tape a 9-volt buzzer that produces a constant frequency of about 1,000 Hz to the bottom of an empty plastic pail. You can buy a buzzer in a radio or electronics store. Attach a light rope to the handle of the pail and ask a friend to swing the pail over his or her head while you listen to the sound some distance away. How does the sound as the buzzer is approaching you differ from the sound you hear when the buzzer is moving away from you? Can you explain why the sounds differ? How are the pitches you hear affected by the speed at which the buzzer is moving?

You can make a model of this effect (known as the Doppler effect) with the water tank you used in Experiment 3.2. Set up the tank as you did in that experiment with pieces of soft cloth lining the inner sides of the tank. Make waves by dipping your finger at a constant rate into the water in the center of the tank. As you can see, the circular waves spread outward and the wavelength is constant. Now, move your finger to one end of the tank and again make waves at a constant rate. But this time, as you make the waves, move your finger toward the opposite end of the tank. How does the wavelength of the waves in the direction your finger is moving compare with the wavelengths of the waves in the opposite direction?

At which end of the tank will more waves arrive per second? In other words, at which end of the tank will the frequency of the waves be greater?

How does this experiment with waves in the water tank help to explain the Doppler effect?

EXPLORING ON YOUR OWN

Who was Christian Johann Doppler? What mathematical relationship did he find relating the pitch of a sound to the relative motion of the sound's source and the listener? Does the same relationship hold for light?

How is the Doppler effect used in burglar alarms?

From Hose Telephones to Sound Effects

This chapter is a potpourri (mixture) of experiments and activities related to sound. You will discover how to make a telephone from garden hoses, how to select certain sounds from a noisy room, absorb unwanted sounds, measure sound intensities in decibels and other units, focus on one sound among many, build a simple wire harp and wind chimes, identify animal and other common sounds, and try your skill at developing various sound effects.

5.1 A Hose Telephone

Materials:
- 2 or more garden hoses
- a friend
- 2 funnels

Although air is not the best conductor of sound, sound waves reflected within a long, narrow, air-filled tube can be used to carry your voice over surprising distances. In fact, you could build an intercom system for your home using garden hoses.

To see how this might be done, join two or more garden hoses together. Speak softly into one end of the hose while a friend holds the other end of the hose against his or her ear. Can your friend hear what you are saying? Ask your friend to speak into the hose while you listen at the other end. Can you hear your friend?

Can you use the hoses as a short-distance telephone?

Is the sound transmission improved if you speak into a funnel inserted into the end of the hose? Is the transmission improved if you listen with your ear against a funnel inserted into the end of hose?

While you have a long hose and funnels, listen to the sound you can make by pursing your lips making a razzberry sound with them as you blow into one end of a hose. How is the sound affected if you put a funnel into the end of the hose from which the sound emerges?

5.2 Pipes of Pan

Pan was an ancient Greek god of shepherds and their flocks. He played a musical instrument made of a series of pipes of different lengths, sometimes called a panpipe today.

Materials:
- cardboard tubes
- tape
- board
- a place where there are many different sounds
- conch shells of different size (optional)

Prepare a number of cardboard tubes of different length. You might cut lengths of 1.0 m, 0.8 m, 0.6 m, 0.4 m, 0.2 m, and 0.1 m from mailing tubes. (Alternatively, you can cut lengths of 3 ft, 2.5 ft, 2 ft, 1.5 ft, 1 ft, and 6 in from the same tubing.) Tape the tubes of different length to a single long board, as shown in Figure 25.

[FIGURE 25]

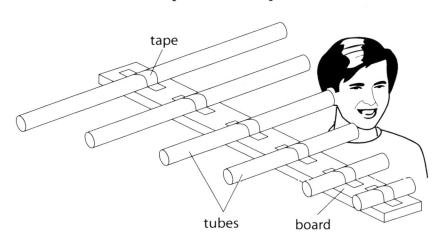

tape

tubes   board

Listen to the sounds you hear through the Pipes of Pan.

Take the tubes to a place where there are lots of different sounds, such as a busy classroom, a workshop, or a noisy street. Put your ear, in turn, against each of the different length tubes. How do the sounds you hear from the different tubes compare? How can you explain the differences in the sounds you hear? Remember what you learned about resonance!

In Experiment 6.2, you will learn how to make a panpipe that resembles the original. It will be one that you can actually play.

People often say that when you hold a conch shell against your ear, you can hear the sea somehow mysteriously stored within the shell. Now that you have learned about resonance and investigated the Pipes of Pan, how can you explain the mystery? What do you really hear when you put your ear to a conch shell? How can you test your explanation by using conch shells of different sizes?

Materials:

- thin-walled, rigid plastic tubing ($\frac{1}{2}$-inch in diameter) or an old garden hose
- caps to fit plastic tubing, or tape and coins to cover end of garden hose, or modeling clay to seal either
- cotton
- pencil or drinking straw
- soft fabric, such as facial tissue or toilet paper
- small metal nuts or washers
- windup alarm clock that makes a loud ticking sound
- Styrofoam ice chest
- soft towels
- other materials to absorb sound
- heavy string
- various materials such as newspaper, cardboard, tablecloth, towels, curtains, wood, concrete, Styrofoam, and acoustical tiles

Have you ever eaten in a restaurant or cafeteria where the noise level was so loud that you had trouble carrying on a conversation? The next time you find yourself in such a place, look at the walls, ceiling, and floor of the room. Then compare them with another public eating place where the noise level is much lower. Some materials absorb sound better than others, and are poor reflectors of sound.

To see how a substance can absorb sound, make a tube about 10 cm (4 in) long from a piece of $\frac{1}{2}$-inch diameter, thin-walled, rigid plastic tubing, or cut a similar length from a piece of old garden hose. If you use garden hose, **ask an adult** to cut the hose with a sharp knife. Whichever tube you choose, seal one end. Often plastic tubing is sold with caps so you can make tubes of various lengths. Garden hose can be sealed by taping a coin such as a penny over one end. Either type of tube can also be sealed with a lump of modeling clay.

Blow into or across the open end of the tube to produce a clear, high-pitched sound. Now place a small piece of cotton into the tube. Push it gently to the bottom of the tube above the cap with a pencil or drinking straw. Again, blow into the tube. Why is there no sound?

Try placing a soft material such as facial tissue or toilet paper into the tube. How do these materials affect the sound you get by blowing into the tube? Next, place small metal nuts or washers in the tube. How do they affect the sound?

Find an old windup alarm clock that makes a loud ticking sound and a Styrofoam ice chest. Set the alarm to go off momentarily and place the clock in the ice chest. How much of the sound would you estimate comes through the chest? Repeat the experiment, but this time line the ice chest with soft towels and cover the clock with the same material. How does this affect the sound you hear? Try other materials. Which material seems to be the best sound absorber?

Hang the clock from a long heavy string. Place your ear about a foot away from the clock. Have a friend place different materials between your ear and the clock. Why should all the materials be of the same size?

Some of the materials you might try include newspaper, cardboard, tablecloth, towels, curtains, wood, concrete, Styrofoam, and acoustic tiles.

Design an experiment to find out how thickness affects the ability of a material to absorb sound.

EXPLORING ON YOUR OWN

Make this experiment much more quantitative by using a sound meter.

What is reverberation time? What role does it play in designing lecture halls, auditoriums, and theaters?

Investigate acoustic tiles. How are they built to absorb sound? What fraction of the sound that falls on them is absorbed?

Do some research on automobile mufflers. Do some reading and talk to an automobile mechanic. How do these devices reduce the sounds you hear from the engine of an automobile?

5.4 Intensity of Sound

Materials:

- sound meter
- ear-protecting gear
- a variety of places

As you learned in Experiment 2.2, the human ear is very sensitive to sound. At the limit, or the threshold, of hearing (the smallest detectable sound), the human ear can detect intensities as small as a trillionth of a watt per square meter (W/m^2). The scale used to measure the intensity of sound (loudness) has its zero value at the threshold of hearing. The unit used to measure loudness is the bel (B), named in honor of Alexander Graham Bell, who is credited with inventing the telephone. More commonly, scientists use the decibel (dB), which is one-tenth of a bel. When the intensity of a sound, as measured in W/m^2, increases by ten times, the measurement in bels increases by 1 B or 10 dB.

Table 2 gives the intensity of various common sounds as measured in bels, decibels, watts per square meter, and intensity relative to the threshold of hearing.

Use a sound meter to measure the intensity of sound in different places. **Wear ear-protecting gear while testing near noisy places.** In addition to the places listed in Table 2, you might try a busy classroom, a classroom during a test, a playground, a baseball or football stadium after the home team scores and after the visiting team scores, your house at night and at breakfast, and other noisy and quiet areas.

Table 2: Intensities of different sounds

Source of Sound	Intensity of sound in B	Intensity of sound in dB	Intensity of sound in W/m²	Intensity compared to threshold of hearing
threshold of hearing	0	0	1 trillionth	1
rustling leaves	1	10	10 trillionths	10 times
whispering	2	20	100 trillionths	100 times
normal conversation	4	40	10 billionths	10,000 times
vacuum cleaner	7	70	10 millionths	10 million times
heavy traffic	9	90	1 thousandth	1 billion times
riveter at work	10	100	1 hundredth	10 billion times
loud rock music	12	120	1	1 trillion times
threshold of pain	12	120	1	1 trillion times
jet airplane	15	150	1,000	1 quadrillion times
rocket engine	18	180	1 million	1 quintillion times

5.5 Your Brain as a Sound Filter

Materials:
-radio
-tape recorder
-a friend
-a paragraph or two from an interesting book or magazine article

Most people are able to concentrate on a particular task that requires hearing sounds even in a noisy place. Our brains are able to focus on the sounds we want to hear and ignore other sounds.

To see how this works, tune a radio to a talk station. Then turn on a tape recorder so that you can record sounds through the microphone. Ask a friend to listen carefully while you read him or her a paragraph or two from a book or magazine article that you found to be very interesting. Next, ask your friend to read something to you that you know will interest you.

After you finish the readings, turn off the radio and tape recorder. Ask your friend to recount what was read. Then you can recall what was read to you. You will both probably recall what was read, but will be less able to remember what was on the radio.

Finally, listen to the playback on the tape recorder. The machine has no brain to filter sound. As a result, you and your friend will be more aware of all the background noise that you both ignored during the readings.

5.6 A Wire Harp

Materials:
- wire cutters
- coat hangers
- ruler
- file
- hammer
- staples
- piece of 2-in x 4-in lumber about 20 cm (8 in) long
- pliers
- safety goggles
- an adult

Ask an adult to use wire cutters to cut one or two coat hangers into pieces 10–20 cm (4–8 in) long. Use a file to smooth off the ends. **Wearing safety goggles**, use a hammer and staples to fasten the wires to a piece of 2-in x 4-in lumber about 20 cm long, as shown in Figure 26. How will the sounds produced by plucking the longer wires compare with those generated by plucking the shorter ones? Can you adjust the lengths of the wires so that you can play a simple tune?

What role does the wooden block play in this "harp"? To find out, pluck a wire as you hold it with a pair of pliers. What difference do you notice in the sound when the wire is not attached to the block of wood?

[FIGURE 26]

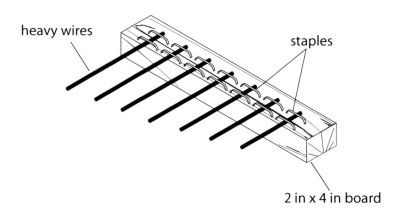

heavy wires

staples

2 in x 4 in board

A wire harp can be made from simple materials. How does the length of the wire affect the sound you hear when you pluck it?

Materials:

- an adult
- pipe cutter or hacksaw
- $\frac{1}{2}$-inch galvanized electrical conduit (from a hardware or electrical supply store)
- electric drill and bits
- string or thin wires
- pieces of wood and nails, or heavy wire, metal stripping, a plastic lid, an old frisbee
- bamboo, strips of wood, wooden dowels, metal scraps, copper pipes, large nails, flowerpots (optional)

Most people enjoy the sounds that come from a set of wind chimes. You can make a set of your own quite easily from lengths of electrical conduit.

Ask an adult to use a pipe cutter or hacksaw to cut some electrical conduit into lengths that vary from 50 cm (20 in) to 20 cm (8 in). **Ask the adult** to drill 3 mm ($\frac{1}{8}$ in) diameter holes across one end of each length of conduit, as shown in Figure 27.

The pieces of conduit can then be suspended by strings or thin wires from a ring or triangle. You can make a triangle by nailing pieces of wood together. A ring can be made from heavy wire, metal stripping, a plastic lid, or an old frisbee.

[FIGURE 27]

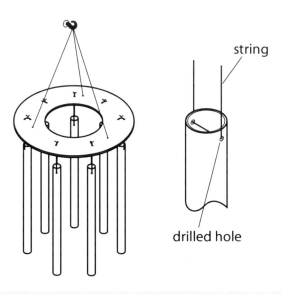

string

drilled hole

A set of wind chimes can be made from electrical conduit, string, and an old frisbee.

If you want the chimes to ring out distinct notes, **ask the adult** to trim the tubes until they generate the notes you like to hear as you assemble the chimes.

You might like to make a variety of wind chimes from various materials. You can use bamboo, strips of wood, wooden dowels, metal scraps, copper pipes, large nails, or flowerpots.

Materials:
-tape recorder
-animals—pets, birds,
  frogs, peepers, crickets,
  squirrels, farm animals,
  etc.

Use a tape recorder to record as many animal sounds as you can. You might begin with your own pets if you have a dog, cat, or another pet that makes sounds. If you wake up early, you can probably record a number of different bird calls.

Early spring is a good time to pick up the sounds of croaking frogs and peeper frogs. In the fall, you can capture the sounds of crickets. Can you find other insects that make sounds?

Squirrels are very common in most places where there are trees. They can usually figure out a way to get the seeds from your bird feeder, but do they make any sounds? If they do, try to record them.

If you live near a farm or can visit one in the country, you may be able to record the cows mooing, a horse's whinny, ducks quacking, chickens clucking, and sheep bleating. What other animal sounds can you record?

You are more likely to hear birds than see them. Can you identify different birds from the "songs" they sing?

You might play your recordings for friends and family. How many of the animals can they identify?

EXPLORING ON YOUR OWN

You may have heard that humpback whales sing. You may even have heard a record of their songs. Do these whales always sing the same song or does their song change? Do other species of whales sing? Do they make sounds?

Barn owls have a keen sense of hearing. Find out how these birds use their ears to hunt.

Materials:
- a number of different people
- common objects that produce a sound when they are dropped
- piece of plywood about 60 cm (2 ft) on a side to protect floor

Many objects have a natural frequency of vibration that people readily identify when they hear it. Try testing different people to see if they recognize common sounds. Have them listen with their eyes closed while you drop different objects on a piece of plywood covering a portion of a floor. You might include a book, a spoon, a newspaper, a ball, and a number of other common objects that can be dropped without breaking. Can anyone hear a pin drop?

Score your subjects on the basis of the percentage of sounds they correctly identify. Are older people more successful than younger people in identifying sounds? Are girls better able to identify sounds than boys are?

EXPLORING ON YOUR OWN

If your school has an audio-frequency generator, ask your science teacher if you can use it to test the ability of people to hear various frequencies of sound. The range of frequencies that humans can hear extends from 20 to 20,000 Hz (vibrations per second). What percentage of the people you test can hear the entire range? Does age or gender affect the ability to hear different frequencies?

Design an experiment to determine the frequency range of the human voice. How does it compare with the frequency range we can hear? Is it related to age or gender? If it is, how is it related?

Materials:
- tape recorder
- heavy cellophane
- Styrofoam coffee cups
- rice
- Ping-Pong ball
- water
- hose
- wood
- sheet metal
- wax-coated paper cups

You can have a lot of fun making sounds that resemble those you hear in the real world. The easiest way to produce sound effects that can be used in a school play or a radio program is to record the actual sounds with a tape recorder and then play them at the appropriate times. The most challenging way is to make these sounds by using your voice. With practice and lots of listening as well, you can imitate voices of friends and famous people you hear on television, radio, and in movies. But imitating sounds—a creaking door, galloping horses, gunfire, a motorcycle engine, breaking glass, thunder—is more difficult and may require using devices that generate sounds similar to the real ones.

By crinkling heavy cellophane, you can make sounds that resemble a fire. Gentler crinkling can generate a sound that resembles food frying in a pan. A sound effect resembling galloping horses can be made by holding Styrofoam coffee cups horizontally and rubbing the open ends up and down over one another. Rice falling on a Ping-Pong ball sounds like rain, but the sound will need amplification. Spraying water onto a wooden surface may be better.

Thunder can be simulated by suspending a long thin piece of sheet metal and sending wavelike motions along its length. Turning a wax-coated paper cup held at an angle inside an identical cup can produce squeaking sounds that suggest the opening of doors in a haunted house.

Use your own ingenuity to develop your own sound effects for the sounds discussed above and for others.

THE SOUNDS OF MUSIC

As you learned, resonance is a reinforcement or intensifying of a sound that occurs when certain conditions are met. You have seen that tubes and strings will resonate to sounds of a particular wavelength. The standing waves established in tubes and strings due to resonance is one of the fundamental principles of music. But why does a column of air resonate when it has a particular length?

To answer that question, look at Figure 28a. The length of the column of air in the tube can be adjusted by moving the tube up or down in the water. A vibrating tuning fork, or any vibrating object, including a simple pendulum, moves back and forth with a particular frequency. In so doing, it produces a sound wave. When the lower prong of the tuning fork moves downward, it creates a region of compression in the air. That compression moves down the tube and is reflected back up after striking the water at the bottom of the tube. For that upward moving compression to make the sound grow louder, as happens when there is resonance, it must strike the prong when it is moving upward. This will help move the prong and make stronger compressions.

The prong's motion during one cycle, when it makes one wavelength, is shown in Figure 28b. It moves downward from a to 0 to b and then upward from b to 0 and back to a. For resonance to occur, the compression (the crest of the wave if viewed as a transverse wave) must travel down the tube and back again while the prong makes half a vibration—from a to 0 to b. As it begins the second half of its vibration, from b to 0 and back to a, it should receive help from the reflected compression that it started during the first half of the cycle. The sound wave, therefore, must travel half a wavelength to reinforce the motion of the prong, which has gone through half a cycle and created half a wavelength. Consequently, the tube must have a length equal to $1/4$ of the wavelength created by the vibrating prong. Remember, the wave has to travel down the tube and back again. Therefore, the distance down the tube and back up must be half a wavelength. Consequently, the tube's length must be $1/4$ of a wavelength. In the time that the prong makes one complete vibration, the sound wave would travel four times the length of the tube.

As Figure 28c shows, the closed end of the tube will be a node; the open end will be an antinode. Of course, as Figure 28d and 28e reveal, the same tube could also be $3/4$ of a wavelength, $5/4$ of a wavelength, and so on. The sound with a wavelength four times that of the tube is called the fundamental note. It is the lowest note that resonates. The other notes with shorter wavelengths and higher frequencies or pitch are called overtones or harmonics. When you blow into a tube you can sometimes change the note by blowing harder or softer. The lowest note you can obtain is the fundamental. The notes with higher pitch are the overtones.

Musical instruments that produce notes by the resonance of air in tubes are called wind instruments. These, in turn, are subdivided into woodwinds and brasses.

[FIGURE 28]

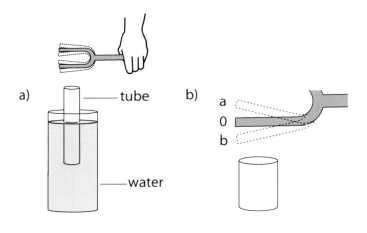

a)   — tube   b)

          — water

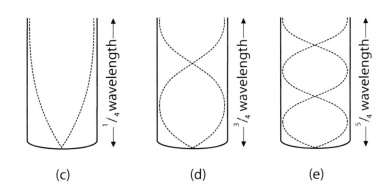

(c)   (d)   (e)

a) A vibrating object can produce standing sound waves in a tube closed at one end. b) The vibrating object can establish standing waves if the reflected waves push the vibrating object so as to reinforce its motion. c) The tube will resonate if its length is 1/4 the wavelength of the sound wave entering it. d) and e) The tube will also resonate if it is 3/4, 5/4, 7/4, etc. of the wavelength of the sound wave entering it.

Woodwinds, which may be made of wood or metal, include such instruments as the flute, clarinet, saxophone, and bassoon. Except for the flute, these instruments have a reed in the mouthpiece. The flute is played by blowing across the mouth hole. Instruments classified as brasses include the cornet, French horn, trumpet, trombone, and tuba. They are played with the player's lips vibrating against the mouthpiece.

Materials:

-thin-walled, rigid plastic tubing ($\frac{1}{2}$-inch diameter) or an old garden hose, or wide-diameter drinking straws

-metric ruler

-sharp scissors or a sharp knife (if a knife is used to cut garden hose, ask an adult to help you)

-water

Use sharp scissors to cut off two pieces of thin-walled, rigid plastic tubing. One piece should be about 10 cm (4 in) long, the other about 30 cm (12 in) long. If you cannot find plastic tubing, have **an adult** use a sharp knife to cut off pieces of old garden hose of about the same lengths. You might also try wide-diameter drinking straws; however, it is more difficult to obtain clear notes by blowing into straws.

Close one end of the short tube by holding your thumb or finger tightly against the opening. Then blow into the other end. You should be able to make a sound with a distinct pitch. If you have trouble making a clear sound, be sure you have the other end of the tube completely closed. If that does not work, try changing the position of the tube relative to your lips, or try blowing harder or softer. You will eventually succeed in making a clear note.

Repeat the experiment, using the long tube. How is the sound from this tube different than the sound from the shorter tube? Which tube produces a sound with the higher pitch? With which tube can you change the pitch of the sound by blowing harder or softer?

Hold the longer tube under a faucet and fill it with water. Let about a quarter of the water flow out of the tube. Then blow into the tube. Note the pitch of the sound

[FIGURE 29]

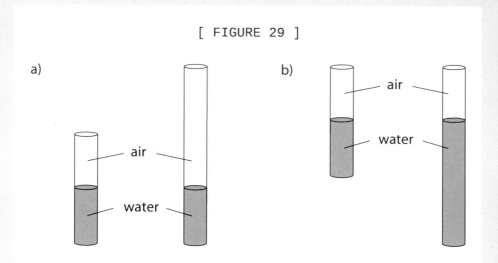

a)

air

water

b)

air

water

When you blow into the tubes that are partially filled with water, how will the sounds compare in (a)? In (b)?

you hear. Release more water and blow into the tube again. What happens to the pitch of the sound as the amount of water in the tube decreases? Can you explain why?

Look at the drawings in Figure 29. How will the sounds you make by blowing into the two tubes shown in (a) compare? How will the sounds you make by blowing into the two tubes shown in (b) compare? If you do not know, try the experiment and find out.

Materials:

- thin-walled, rigid plastic tubing (¹/₂-inch diameter) or an old garden hose, or wide-diameter drinking straws
- sharp scissors or knife (if a knife is used, ask an adult to help you)
- metric ruler
- petroleum jelly
- coins
- masking tape
- sheet of cardboard

As you saw in Chapter 5, a panpipe is an ancient musical instrument. It was originally made from reeds or bamboo. You can make one by using thin-walled, rigid plastic tubing or pieces of an old garden hose. By making such a musical instrument you will find out how the length of a closed tube is related to the frequency of the sound it can produce.

If you make the panpipe from plastic tubing, the tubes can be cut with sharp scissors. The same is true of drinking straws that have a large diameter; however, it is more difficult to obtain clear notes by blowing into straws. If you use an old garden hose, **ask an adult** to cut the lengths you need with a sharp knife.

To make a panpipe that will play the scale—do, re, me, fa, so, la, ti, do—cut the tubing into the following lengths: 15.0 cm, 13.4 cm, 12.1 cm, 11.3 cm, 10.0 cm, 8.9 cm, 7.9 cm, and 7.2 cm. If the plastic tubing comes with caps, you can use them to close off the lower end of each tube.

If you use garden hose to make the tubes, have **an adult** cut the hose into tubes of the same lengths. To close off one end of each tube, first coat the rubber or plastic at the end of each tube with a thin layer of petroleum jelly. Be careful not to get any petroleum jelly on the side of the tube. Next, place a coin on the petroleum jelly. Then tape the coin securely and firmly in place with strips of masking tape.

You can be sure that a tube is properly sealed at one end if you get a clear note when you blow sharply across the open end of the tube. If you have a keen ear for music, you may want to adjust the lengths of the tubes slightly to obtain just the right pitch.

Place the tubes side by side in order of decreasing length on a sheet of cardboard, as shown in Figure 30. Use masking tape to fasten the tubes to the cardboard. Be sure the open ends of the tubes project a short distance above the cardboard. Now see if you can play simple tunes by blowing across the tubes.

[FIGURE 30]

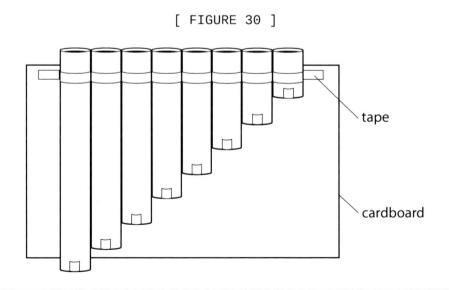

tape

cardboard

You can make a panpipe and use it to play simple tunes.

How is the length of the closed tube related to the pitch (frequency) of the sound that it makes when you blow across it?

Does the length of the tube affect how hard you have to blow to make a note? If it does, can you explain why?

EXPLORING ON YOUR OWN

Build a panpipe by using test tubes. The lengths of the tubes can be adjusted by adding water to the tubes. Can you build a similar panpipe by using soda bottles?

6.3 A Slide Trombone

Materials:

-length of garden hose or thin-walled plastic tubing about 30 cm (12 in) long

-a length of wooden dowel about 30 cm (12 in) long that just fits inside the hose or tubing

-petroleum jelly

-tall jar of water

With the panpipe that you made in Experiment 6.2, you played different notes by blowing into closed tubes of different lengths. Another way to produce different notes is to change the length of the tube by sliding a long dowel different distances into the tube. You will need a length of garden hose or thin-walled plastic tubing about 30 cm long and a comparable length of wooden dowel that just fits inside the hose. Coat the end of the dowel with petroleum jelly to make it easier to move and to provide a seal between the hose and the dowel.

Blow across the open end of the hose or tubing to produce a note. From what you learned by making a panpipe, predict what will happen to the pitch (frequency) of the sound if you move the dowel farther into the hose, thus shortening the length of the tube. What will happen to the pitch if you pull more of the dowel out of the hose, thus increasing the length of the tube?

Now, test your predictions. Were they correct?

Can you play a tune on your homemade "trombone"?

Place one end of the hose or tubing near the bottom of a tall jar of water, as shown in Figure 31. Produce a note of a certain pitch by blowing into the tube. Predict what will happen if, as you blow into the tube, you increase the length of the air column inside the tube by slowly raising the tube upward in the water. What will happen if you decrease the length of the air column by slowly lowering the tube into the water? Were your predictions correct?

[FIGURE 31]

length of garden hose
or plastic tubing

tall container of water

What happens to the pitch of the note you hear when
you lower the tube deeper into the water as you blow
into the tube? What happens as you raise the tube while
blowing into it?

6.4 A Bottle or Glass Band

Materials:

-plastic soda bottles of different volumes—2-liter or $^1/_2$ gallon, 1-liter or 1-quart, $^1/_2$-liter or 1-pint

-water

-a number of friends

-glass bottles and/or drinking glasses of different size

-spoon

Gather together a number of plastic soda bottles of different volumes—2-liter or $^1/_2$ gallon, 1-liter or 1-quart, $^1/_2$-liter or 1-pint. You know that if you blow gently across the mouth of these bottles, the air inside will vibrate and emit a sound of a distinct pitch. By partially filling the bottles with water, you can reduce the length of the air column. From what you have learned in previous experiments, predict the effect of shortening or lengthening the air column on the frequency (pitch) of the sound produced.

By varying the size of the bottles and the volume of water you pour into them, you can produce all the notes of a scale—do, re, me, fa, so, la, ti, do. If you succeed in making the first "do" note, what should you do to the length of the air column to make the "re" note?

Together with some friends, each of whom can play one or two of the notes by blowing across the mouths of the bottles, your "bottle band" can play some simple tunes.

You can prepare a similar "glass band" by gathering glass bottles or drinking glasses of different size. By partially filling the different size bottles or glasses with varying volumes of water, you can obtain a variety of notes by gently tapping on the vessels with a spoon. Which bottles or glasses produce notes with the higher frequencies (pitch)? Which generate notes of lower pitch? Can you explain why the results are the opposite of what you found when you blew into the bottles? What do you think is vibrating to produce sounds of a distinct frequency now? How can you be sure?

Materials:
- an adult
- saw
- pine board, 30 cm x 38 cm (12 in x 15 in)
- ruler
- pencil
- hammer
- 8 small nails
- 10 screw eyes
- large nail
- nylon fishing line
- scissors
- a piece of 1.9-cm (³/₄-in)-thick pine board, 60 cm x 5 cm (24 in x 2 in)
- saw
- 2 Popsicle sticks or wooden coffee stirrers

An Ear Harp

Ask an adult to cut a pine board that is 30 cm x 38 cm (12 in x 15 in). Draw a line near one edge of the 30 cm side of the board that is parallel to the edge. Draw a slanting line starting at one corner of the opposite side, as shown in Figure 32. Using a hammer, drive eight evenly spaced small nails halfway into the wood along the line parallel to the edge of the board.

Insert eight evenly spaced screw eyes partway into the wood along the slanted line. You can use a large nail and a hammer to make small holes where you plan to place the screw eyes. The holes will make it easier to start the screw eyes.

[FIGURE 32]

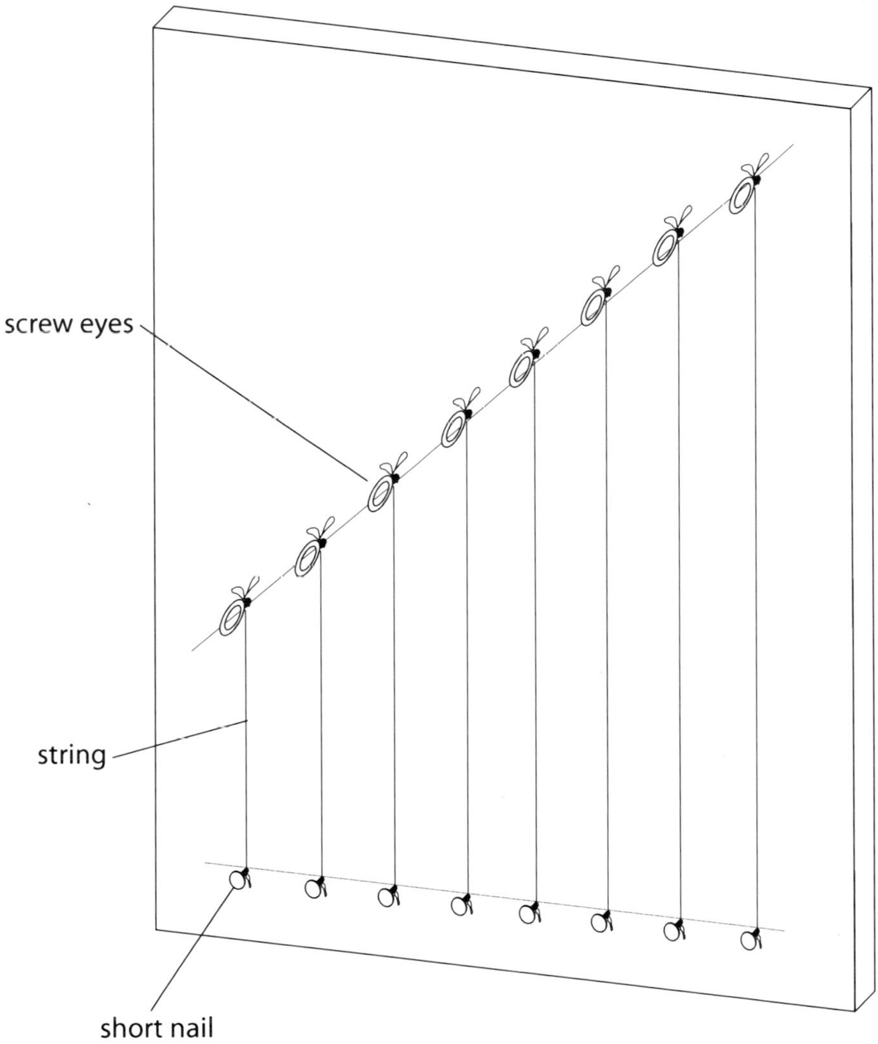

screw eyes

string

short nail

An ear harp can be made from nails, screw eyes, fishing line, and a board.

Tie a length of nylon fishing line to each nail. Tie the opposite ends of these lines tightly to the bases of the corresponding screw eyes. The strings can be tightened further by turning the screw eyes. If needed, a large nail can be used as a lever to turn the screw eyes. The strings can be tuned by tightening or loosening the screw eyes.

Hold the back of the harp next to your ear as you play tunes on it by plucking the strings. How does the length of the string affect the pitch (frequency) of the sound the string makes when you pluck it? How does increasing or decreasing tension in the string affect the pitch of the note it produces? Other than holding nails and screw eyes in position, what is the purpose of the board?

A One-String Guitar

Ask an adult to cut a piece of 1.9-cm ($^3/_4$-in)-thick pine board to a length of 60 cm (24 in) and a width of 5 cm (2 in). Insert a screw eye partway into the wood, about 2 cm (1 in) from each end of the board, as shown in Figure 33. About 4 cm (1 $^1/_2$ in) from each end of the

[FIGURE 33]

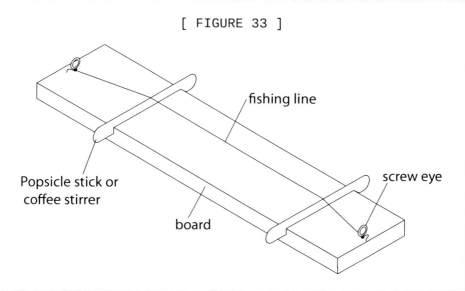

fishing line

Popsicle stick or
coffee stirrer

screw eye

board

A one-string guitar can be made from simple materials.

board, saw a groove about 0.5 cm ($^1/_4$ in) deep across the width of the board. Insert a Popsicle stick or wooden coffee stirrer into each groove. Connect the bases of the two screw eyes with a length of nylon fishing line. Tighten the instrument's string by turning the screw eyes. A large nail can be used as a lever if you cannot tighten the string sufficiently by hand.

To play the instrument, use a finger of one hand to press the string against the wood at different places along the board between the two Popsicle sticks while you pluck the string with your other hand. By marking the points where pressing the string provides a clear note, you can play a number of simple tunes on your guitar.

How does the length of the string that is free to vibrate when you pluck it affect the pitch (frequency) of the sound it produces? What can you do to amplify the sound coming from the instrument?

EXPLORING ON YOUR OWN

Build a musical instrument of your own design.

Further Reading

Books

Carlson, Laurie. *Thomas Edison for Kids: His Life and Ideas with 21 Activities*. Chicago: Chicago Review Press, 2006.

DiSpezio, Michael A. *Awesome Experiments in Light and Sound*. New York: Sterling Publications, 2006.

Ebner, Aviva, Ph.D. *Physical Science Experiments*. New York: Chelsea House Publishers, 2011.

Green, Dan. *Physics: What Matter Matters*. New York: Kingfisher, 2009.

Holihan, Kerrie Logan. *Isaac Newton and Physics for Kids: His Life and Ideas with 21 Activities*. Chicago: Chicago Review Press, 2009.

Kessler, Colleen. *A Project Guide to Sound*. Hockessin, Del.: Mitchell LanePublishers, 2011.

Robinson, Tim. *The Everything Kids' Science Magical Experiments Book*. Avon, Mass. Adams Media, 2007.

Internet Addresses

101Science.com. *Physics*.
<http://www.101science.com/physics.htm>

Science Kids. *Cool Physics Science Fair Project Ideas*.
<http://www.sciencekids.com.nz/projects/physics.html>

INDEX

W

wavelength, 46, 47
water waves, 61–68, 85
  diffraction of, 67–68, 85
  reflection of, 62–65
  refraction of, 65–66
waves
  as a model for sound,
    38–55
  frequency and
    wavelength, 51
  from a pendulum, 53–55

longitudinal, 45–46, 52,
  56, 70
  pulse of air, 39
  standing, 49–51, 57, 60
  transverse, 47–49
wind chimes, 101–102
wind instruments, 52, 108
  closed tubes, 110–112
wire harp, 99